Malmesbury Reflections

A pictorial history

Malmesbury Civic Trust

Published by
Malmesbury Civic Trust
Chalcourt, Dark Lane, Malmesbury, SN16 0BB

Printed by
CPI Antony Rowe
Bumpers Farm, Chippenham, Wiltshire SN14 6LH

Fonts: Title, Harrington provided by Fontsempire.co; Text, Arial

Front Cover: A postcard showing the railway station with the Abbey in the background c1905.

Back Cover: A postcard showing the top of the High Street, Market Cross and Hospital c1900 together with the same view in July 2020 showing the bollards to allow pedestrians extra space and a man queueing outside No 9A Barbers during the Covid-19 crisis.

ISBN 978-0-9536692-6-4

Introduction and acknowledgments

This has been written during the Covid-19 pandemic which has not only caused great suffering and sometimes death for those catching the disease but also great disruption to all of our lives. On 23rd March everyone was directed to stay at home except for essential purposes and most shops had to close. Since 4th July restrictions have gradually been lifted but increases in the number of new infections has paused and sometimes reversed these relaxations. The result has been a global economic recession. Locally Dyson announced in July 450 redundancies at its Malmesbury Headquarters. It is likely other local businesses will not survive. The town may look different in future.

Obliged to remain at home for more than three months many took the opportunity to sort through family photographs benefitting the Malmesbury Now and Then Facebook group. Thanks are due to the group administrators Alison Cross-Jones, Hay Blake, Sue Savine and John Slater for overseeing this activity. Alison has also organised all of the publicity. Many new contributors and book orders have come from the group - Karen Selby has channelled the orders. The faith of subscribers who bought in advance is much appreciated.

Many people have collaborated in the production of this book. Photographs from the following have been used and grateful thanks is extended to them:

Now & Then members including Nicola Gilmore (her father was Jim Gilmore, a local journalist for many years), David Shelley, Lynette Babidge, Corinne Ratcliffe (Gastons Dairy), Sarah Cullen, Christine White, Mark Clark, Dr Nigel Pickering, Sue White, Alby Anderson, Jon England (who also obtained permission from Historic England), Mark Westmacott, Norman Tapp, Dave Poole, Jennie Brock and Derek Tilney.

Chris Harvey (Fire Brigade & his son Louis' motorsport career), John Smith (Bowls), Mike Rees (Boxing), Stephen Jepson (Cricket), Jason Bradley (Stop Line Green), Dave Picter (Football), Sue Alexander and Matt Wigley (skateboarding). Photos found on the internet from Colin Hicks, Coach Farmer, Moonraker, the Royal Wiltshire Yeomanry Association and Wiltshire Police.

Graham Carey and colleagues for the 1964 Malmesbury Civic Trust collection. Keith Rayner for his 1999 Malmesbury Civic Trust collection as well as photos of the 1980s and members Gill Rycroft, Roger Griffin, Caroline Pym, Barry and Sheila Dent.

Tristan Forward and his team for the Malmesbury Chronicles of the mid 1980s and Vieve Forward for some of their father, Colin's, photos. The Trustees of the Athelstan Museum and Malmesbury Town Council.

Gordon Williams for images from his own collection. He and Graham Cooke for Bob Browning's archive. David Richards spent time scanning slides and photographs from his mother, Bette's, collection. Liz Snell for many photos and her cousin Linda Hares for information on their families. Helen King for the album showing the rebuilding of Malmesbury Primary School. Ron Bartholomew for a number of colour slides of the 1970s & 80s and Robert Peel for the 2010 Freedom.

Jim Rivett, Olive Kemp, Ted Hitchings, David Jones, Michael Adye, Roger Lewis, David Willis, Christine Schofield, Terry Thomas, John Bowen, Paddy Lockstone, Ted Hall, Sara Crabb, Mollie Raiss, Kim Power and Christine Jones (Boulton's Bakery) who have provided photos over the years.

Thanks are also due to my wife Val, Paul and Frances Smith for proof reading and editing the text.

 A few notes about the book. It complements last year's *Malmesbury Now and Then* - many subjects covered there have been excluded. This is not a comprehensive town history - images of several important organisations and events are missing. The sections are generally arranged in chronological order. There is a brief index which unfortunately does not have space for family names but does include streets, major employers and trades.

Copyright holders, where known, are named on the image together with its date. Where the copyright holder is unknown the image's source is provided with the date of the photograph below.

Charles Vernon   August 2020

athelstan museum
MALMESBURY

Athelstan Museum was founded in 1931, at first run by Malmesbury Borough Council and then North Wiltshire District Council. In 2006 control passed to Friends of Athelstan Museum, now a Charitable Incorporated Organisation called Athelstan Museum, Malmesbury. For most of its life it has been housed in Malmesbury Town Hall. In 2015 it bought the decaying old Moravian Church, Oxford Street now renamed the Rausing Building, which is used for storage, temporary exhibitions and events.

It has an extensive collection of local artefacts which has been enhanced by the purchases in 2015 of Roman coins found at Milbourne and in 2020 of J M W Turner's watercolour of Malmesbury Abbey.

The Covid crisis has severely effected the Museum's income as it has been closed for a considerable period. One half of the net proceeds of this book will be donated to the Museum.

Malmesbury Civic Trust was founded in 1964 to oppose a proposed housing development at Daniels Well. It has since sought to enhance civic pride in the town through *conserving the best and improving the rest.* It has provided many civic amenities, for example by planting trees around the town, establishing the Riverwalk in 1972 and the Jubilee Garden, Abbey Row in 1977. These are maintained by the charity's volunteers.

The society plays an active role in planning, seeking to influence policy by leading the preparation of the Conservation Area policies and participating in the Neighbourhood Plan. All local planning applications are scrutinised and commented on where necessary.

Local history is promoted through their books and other publications, town tours and signs.

Considerable financial support has been provided to Athelstan Museum as well as heritage repairs to the Market Cross, Town Hall, United Reformed Church and Baskerville railings.

Charles Vernon has lived in Malmesbury since 1996. He has been Malmesbury Civic Trust's treasurer for more than 20 years, served on Malmesbury Town Council for 14 years and is the Royal British Legion's Malmesbury branch treasurer. Having been persuaded by the Trust's committee to write a local history book for the Millennium he has authored another six books as well as the Riverwalk booklet. Many town walks have been led by him with his wife, Val and they have taken parties to continental battle sites where Malmesbury men have fought and died.

Subscribers

Nikki Allen
Larry Arredondo
Gill & Philip Ashby
Dave & Sue Ashford
Sheila Avis
Lynette Babidge
Caroline Baker
John & Diana Baldwin
Lynne Ballard
Jim Barnes
Judith Barnes
Milo & Hayleigh Barnes
Cecilia Barrow
Margaret Blackmore
Hay Blake
Bob & Kate Blanden
Tom Blanden
Heather Bown
Tara Blazey
Mike Breach
Jennie & Terry Brock
Mark Brock
Christopher D Brooks
Wendy & David Brooks
Kevin & Kate Brown
Ray & Jackie Brown
Shannon, Liam & Kayla Brown
Pauline Bryant
Ros Bull
Sandra & Julian Butler
Jill & Keith Burr
Doreen Campbell
Mick & Jayne Castle
George & June Cattermole
Peter Cattermole
Joanne Clark
Jon Clark & Tony Andrews
Robin & Judy Clark
Matthew & Kate Cloke
Christine Coleman

Martin Collier
Annette Cowling
David Craddock
Theresa Cresswell
Jackie & Mike Cripps
Alison Cross-Jones
Tony & Diana Crowe
Sarah Cullen (née Pike)
Robin Dare
Bill Davies
Gareth Davies
David Dearn
Mike Dee
John Denley
Barry & Sheila Dent
Brian & Leone Dike
Janet Dine
Sue & Alan Dolman
Alison Drew
Nicola Earle
Jocelyn & Paul England
Jon England
Pamela Forster
David Lorenzo Forward
Greg Forward
Janet Fowler
Steven & Emma Francis
Greta Fraser
Terence Fraser
Deborah Frayling
Julian & Marisa Garry
Jane & Martyn Gatrill
Anne & Mike Goodyer
Lyn & Trev Gould
Carol Gray
Adrian Grey
Stephen Grey
Carol Harding
Linda Hares
Chris & Charlene Harvey

Pat & Dave Harvey
Ann & Geoff Hicks
Cindy & Trevor Hicks
Mark Hills
Bryan & Kathleen Hodder
Dave & Carey Hodges
Fran & Rod Hodges
Sue Holbrook
Mike & Sue Holland
Peter Holroyd
Andrea & Steve Hunt
Brian Hyde
Maureen Jenner-Jones
Lisa Johnson
Jamie Johnstone & Lucy Maslin
Brenda Jones
Wayne & Caroline Jones
Caroline & Leslie King
Danny & George King
Carol & Steffen Knight
Frances Lane
Helen Lee
Julia Lee
Gordon & Ann Lewis
Lawrence Lowes
Clive & Sheila Lyddieth
Jackie Lyons
Gloria & Chris Maggs
Stan Malpass
Trisha Martin
Douglas Matthews
Fiona Matthews
Doris & Joe Mattinson
Yvonne McCoubrey
June McElroy
Gillian McFarlane
Gillian Mander (née Tapp)
Graham & Hilary McDougal
Susan Meader
Valerie Meredith

Subscribers

Nigel Mills
John Mitchell
Kevin Mitchell
Sharon Neal
Anthony Newman
Stephen Newman
Mark Newport & family
Albert Newton
Jeremy & Susan Paget
Lucy Paget
Robin Paget & Alison Pope
Roger & Liz Paget
Samuel Paget
Stan & Judy Paginton
Felicity & Keith Parsons
Dave & Sandra Pell
June Catherine Pickthall
Dave & Marion Picter
Colin Pike
Maureen Pike
Owen Pike
Rita Pike
Trevor & Hilary Pike
Sandra Pockett
Julian Ponting
Linda & Bernard Ponting
Bernard & Lilian Poole
David & Rosemary Poole
George Pound
Jeanette Pound
Sue Pratt
Andrew Ratcliffe
Corinne Ratcliffe
Paul, Sarah & Olivia Reed
Jack Rees
Kristian Rees
Luc Rees
Mike Rees
Raymond Reynolds
Annette Robbins & Aileen Castle

Ann & Bob Roberts-Phare
John & Ann Robinson
Fred Salter
Margaret & Ray Sanderson
Phyllis & Harry Sanderson
Hazel Saunders
Sue Savine
Terry Savine
Arthur Scott
Lena Scully
Joy Seager
Karen Selby (née Westmacott)
Peter Stirling Shadwick
Ed & Olwen Shellard
Julie Shone
Kathy Silvanus-Woodcock
Graham Smith
Oscar & Charlotte Smith
Paul & Frances Smith
Sam Smith & Katie Baker
Elizabeth Snell
Jeanette Snell
David Stallworthy
Paul Starns
Maureen Starr
Ash Stone & Sarah Robinson
Valerie Stoneham
Barry Telling
Richard & Jo Thornbury
Tim Thornbury
Alison Tibenham
Charles & Val Vernon
Dee & Eddie Vincent
Shirley Vizard
Monica Vizor
Nigel & Liz Walker
Chris & Marilyn Walton
Yvonne Ward
Dennis & Sue Webb
Norman & Jackie Webb

Mike & Vicki West
David Westmacott
Keith Westmacott
Mark Westmacott
Mike & Chris Westmacott
Pam Wickham
Sue Wilkins
Gordon & Mari Williams
Tim Williams
John & Sheila Wiltshire
Alan & Gill Woodward
Margaret & Richard Woodward
Trevor Woodward
Gary Wormald

In Memory of

Dave Briers
Daniel Castle
Tom, Esther & Nancy Clancy
Cliff Cowling
Pauline Evans
Colin Forward
Nancy Gaisford
Ann & Jim Gilmore
Ann & Jack Hedges
Bob Hinwood
Joan Hinwood
John Lewis
Fred Mitchell & Diane Mitchell
Robert Pound
Aussie & Marilyn Preston
John & Betty Reeves
Lynn Slater
Iris Telling
Bert Vizor
Peggy Vizor
Miranda Westmacott

Contents

Two aerial photos - below the town centre looking west along Abbey Row in 1932 and right looking north-east towards Milbourne in 1965.

Points to note.

1932 Very few cars are parked in Cross Hayes, E.S.T. Cole's garage and the Town Hall extension both look bright and new. In the bottom centre just to the left of Tower House there are buildings next to the Town Hall's yard. This was the Three Horseshoes pub and blacksmiths. The tank is still on top of the water tower this side of the Abbey. Edwards & Son's coachworks on Holloway is in the lower right hand corner. The Great Western Railway's goods shed can be seen on the right edge near the top. Above the Triangle it is difficult to make out West Street but beyond are open fields which later housed Glovers Court and Hudson Road.

1965 In the centre at the bottom is Linolite with two new looking buildings. The Silk Mill can be seen on the right with the gas works to the left of it. The Bowls Club pavilion stands out next to the green. Cross Hayes has cars parked diagonally (later changed with the intent of creating more space but the wider aisles necessary for vehicles to turn through a right angle resulted in fewer). Additionally there is a bus using the stop amongst the cars. The Avon caravan park provided residential pitches from the 1950s to 1978. There is now more development in Milbourne along the road to Garsdon at the top centre. In 1973 the bypass cut a swathe through the countryside shown by the white line. This removed considerable volumes of traffic from the town centre.

Athelstan Museum
1932

Historic England 1965

Milbourne Lane

Blicks Hill

Avon

caravan park

Railway track

Silk
Mill

Linolite

9

Places of Worship

Athelstan Museum c1885

The west end of the Abbey before its restoration above. It is possible the small carriage belonged to the two Misses Luce who lived in Castle House (now part of the Old Bell). Note there are four dormers, the far two being on Castle House the nearer two on the Bell Inn which has no porch and no decoration around its door. Below and to the right this series of photos could have been taken at any time between 1865 and 1900. This is the north side of the Abbey with the rear of St Michael's House on the left. The spire collapsed towards the end of the 15th Century.

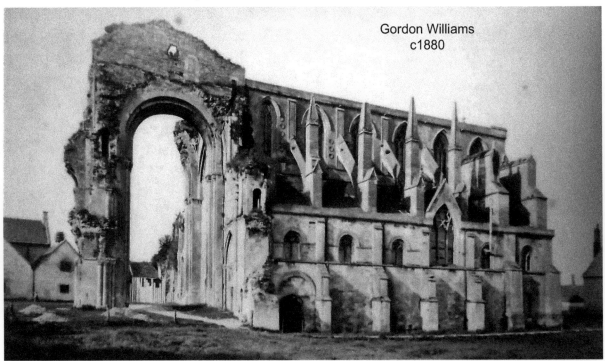

Gordon Williams
c1880

Gordon Williams
c1880

The top view shows the railway line with Abbey House on the skyline. Below the river and Abbey Mill are in the foreground with the water tower and its tank in the centre on the skyline. Today the gardens of houses in Gloucester Road stretch down to Brooky Lane on the riverside. In front of the Abbey are buildings at the foot of the Bell Inn's garden.

Gordon Williams
c1880

Gordon Williams
c1890

The Abbey was built by Norman craftsmen in the 12th Century. At that time few people could read or write so the Church used images to tell the stories of the Bible. Thirty-eight scenes from the Old and New Testaments are depicted on the three upper semi-circles. They begin with the Creation of Adam on the innermost left arch and end with Pentecost on the outer right arch. Maybe to appease former beliefs the lower columns show Virtues conquering Vices, signs of the Zodiac and Labours of the Months. The carvings have weathered considerably since the photograph on the left was taken. The railings were removed c1900.

Below - the interior which has not changed much since 1939. The west end was rebuilt in the first decade of the 20th Century. The interior had a major refurbishment in 1927/8 shown on the next 2 pages. A piece of plaster fell from the ceiling on to the choir stalls in March 1934 and repairs had to be made, completed in November 1935. This was believed to have been caused by the collapse of the tower nearly 400 years before.

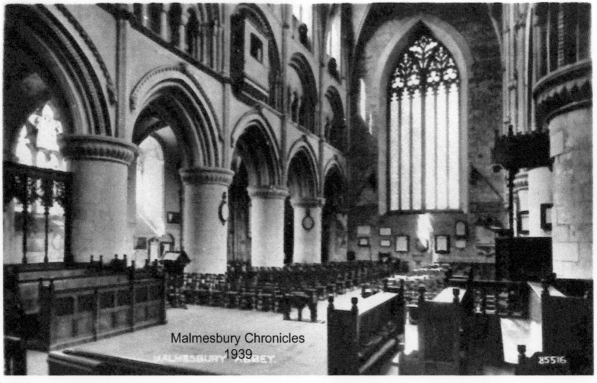

Malmesbury Chronicles
1939

In July 1927 the Abbey was closed to carry out interior work supervised by Harold Brakspear. Note the removal of the stone walls and doorways leading to the main door. The floor was lowered by about a foot revealing the base of the pillars and new under floor heating installed. Gas lighting and coal heating had blackened the stonework which was cleaned.

The next page shows the west end after an unsightly gallery was removed together with the 213 year old Jordan organ, Note the staircase on the floor which provided access to the organ loft. Until 1938 a grand piano provided the music. The west window was reglazed. Deal chairs replaced the pews and the choir desks, pulpit and altar rails renewed. The work was completed in 1929.

Alby Anderson
1927

Alby Anderson
1927

Malmesbury Chronicles 1985

Above Abbey House as seen from the Abbey's roof. Built around 1550 on the undercroft of the 13th Century monastic building, Mr. E. M. Scott Mackirdy owned it for the first half of the 20th Century and made many changes. His widow passed it on to the Deaconess Community of St Andrew from 1968 to 1990. Ian and Barbara Pollard later bought it, opening the gardens to the public in 1998 which have become a major tourist attraction.

On the right the end of terrace house is St Helens, 23 Bristol Street. Once the render had been removed it was identified as a 10th Century single cell chapel. It overlooked the Saxon Kingway which followed Harpers Lane from the Royal estates at Cowage to the town.

Malmesbury Civic Trust 1974

Malmesbury Chronicles 1986

St Mary's Church in the Triangle was rebuilt around 1840 and major internal works completed in 1910. After being used as a classroom during the war the church was closed in 1946. It is used as a community hall and since 2003 has been owned by 1st Malmesbury Scout Group. Their Beavers, Cubs, Scouts and Explorers groups have weekly meetings. A playgroup is shown using it below. Cross Hayes Pre-school moved here in 2010 having previously met in the Town Hall.

Malmesbury Chronicles 1986

Revd. Gawen, who resigned as St Paul's vicar after the Act of Uniformity 1662, is reputed to have founded the Presbyterian (later Congregational) Church in Westport. A chapel was built on a site in St Marys Street about 1689. This was rebuilt in 1788 but that proved to be inadequate, the schoolroom being described as a 'bird loft' from which a child fell. William Stent was commissioned to design a new Church completed in 1867. His drawing on the right employs artistic licence by showing the schoolroom window on the north instead of the south. Two cottages on St Marys Street allowing access *under a low and crumbling archway and along a narrow passage* were bought and demolished A cottage to the north of these, said to be Thomas Hobbes birthplace, was rebuilt. There was seating for 330 with 200 more in the gallery. The modern view below shows fewer seats and the eastern stained glass windows.

Sara Crabb
1867

Malmesbury Civic Trust 2020

Liz Snell
c1900

The manse and Moravian Church on the corner of Oxford Street. The Moravians, the oldest free church, trace their origins here back to the 1740s. A chapel was built in 1770. Although very popular a hundred years ago, the congregation dwindled and the property was sold in 1991. It deteriorated for years until the Church was bought by the Athelstan Museum. It is now called the Julia & Hans Rausing Building. In 2015 the manse was made into two dwellings. The interior of the Church is shown below.

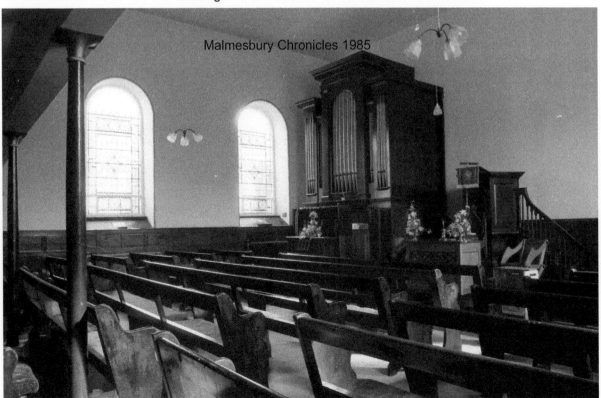

Malmesbury Chronicles 1985

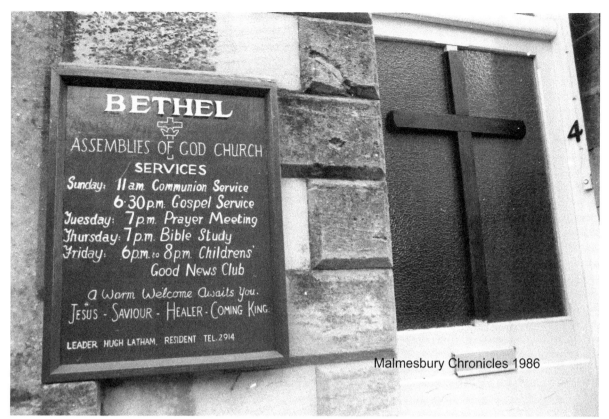

Malmesbury Chronicles 1986

The King's Church, a Pentecostal church, first met in Malmesbury in 1948. In 1986 its first Minister, David Skelton, arranged for the purchase of the old Reading Room, 4 Silver Street. Here they began a Nursery which proved so successful that the church moved in 1997 to the old empty Baptist Chapel, Abbey Row, The Baptist congregation, formed around 1688, built their chapel in 1802 and refurbished in 1910. Unfortunately the date stone has been defaced. By the 1980s the congregation dwindled and the church closed.

Liz Snell
c1930

Athelstan Museum
1926

Malmesbury Chronicles 1985

The parish Church of St Paul's was falling into disrepair when William Stumpe gave the Abbey Church to the town in 1541. What remains is part of the wall on the south side of Birdcage Walk and the steeple housing the bells and clock. In 1926 the steeple required repair. During the Vicar's absence some girls were taken up the scaffolding. Mrs Scott Mackirdy thought this disgraceful, the Vicar agreed and the churchwardens empowered to stop it happening!

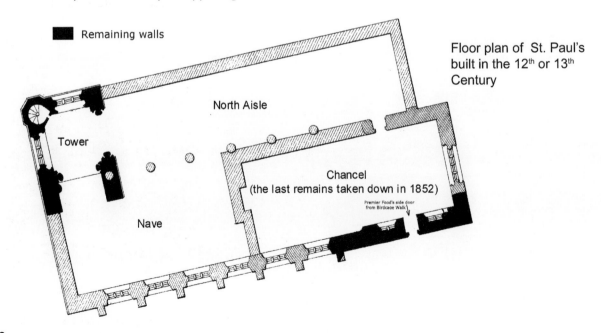

Remaining walls

Floor plan of St. Paul's built in the 12th or 13th Century

North Aisle

Tower

Nave

Chancel
(the last remains taken down in 1852)

Premier Food's side door
from Birdcage Walk

The Primitive Methodists built their first chapel in Bristol Street, next to No. 46. Later used as a garage and warehouse, seen above with its roof covered by tarpaulin and a corrugated iron awning on the right over the entrance. It is now a house. Below the larger chapel built in 1899 at the Triangle which closed in 2004. The photo also shows the old road junction, the paper shop with sub Post Office, Waine's butchers and Avon Bakery.

Malmesbury Civic Trust 2020

Malmesbury Civic Trust 1964

The Independent Church was formed in 1796 and soon moved into two cottages in Silver Street. In 1848, now known as the Ebenezer Chapel, the building was enlarged. After several attempts the church was merged with the Westport Congregationalists in 1952. It became the Masonic Hall in 1958. The small graveyard at the rear is shown above right.

Below a view of St Aldhelms Church from Cross Hayes showing the wall of the original church.

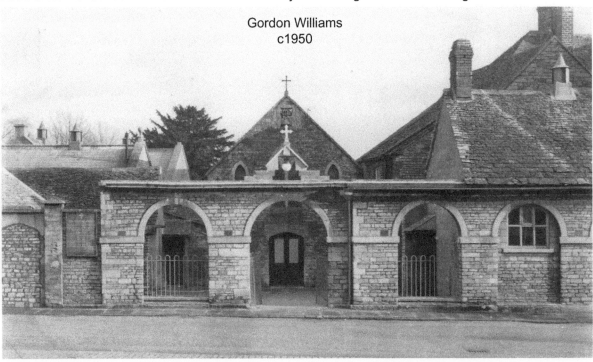

Gordon Williams
c1950

Malmesbury Chronicles 1985

After the Reformation there was no Roman Catholic church here until Charles Dewall gifted Cross Hayes House in 1865. The original church was built along Cross Hayes but this quickly became too small so St Aldhelm's Church was built behind it and the old building converted into St Joseph's School. Below is the rear of Cross Hayes House, used as a convent for nuns who taught at the school 1870-1990, together with the sacristy.

Malmesbury Civic Trust
c1965

Education

Malmesbury Civic Trust 2020

Malmesbury Chronicles 1986

The Old Courthouse above is approached from St Johns Street through the School Arch - so called because the Corporation's School for the sons of Commoners was held here. From at least 1629 to 1888 this was a free school with the expenses paid by the Burgesses and later by a charity set up by Michael Wickes who is commemorated by a plaque on the end of the Almshouses. In the 19th Century between 60 and 70 boys attended but many helped their farming families in the summer.

In 1634 Robert Arch left income from land to be used for the good of the borough. In 1834 £34 was used to run a free girl's school in the Abbey parvise. Capacity was limited to 45 and the school moved to the vestry with 60 pupils. However attendance dropped to around 20 and the school closed about 1886.

Malmesbury Civic Trust 2020

Elizabeth Hodges left £30 a year for education which from 1730 provided was a school for 15 poor boys. In 1836 Jeremiah Webb bought 40 Gloucester Street (above) where he ran the school until 1869. The *National Society for Promoting the Education of the poor in the Principles of the Established Church* had a boys school in Oxford Street around 1820. This was popular and the Church was pleased to be given land in Crab Tree Close where a new Boys School was built in 1857 (below). This moved to the old Grammar School site in 1966.

Malmesbury Civic Trust 1964

Malmesbury Civic Trust
1903

The National Society decided to offer education to girls and in 1857 a new school was built in Cross Hayes. The costs were borne by Samuel Brook of Cowbridge House and his nephew Revd. Charles Kemble. It could accommodate 300 pupils aged between 5 and 14. The subjects were reading, writing, arithmetic and needlework. By the 1960s one of the two doorways shown on the right above had been filled in and the other made into a window.

Christine White
1961

Malmesbury Civic Trust 2020

In 1966 the Girls (then mixed Infants) and Boys (mixed Junior) Schools were combined and moved to the old Grammar School on Tetbury Hill. Six years later the Cross Hayes building became the Library. Since 1926 the County Council has provided books for the Library initially run by the Borough Council in the Town Hall. After the war the County took full control at 44 High Street. The Cross Hayes premises were bigger and used to coordinate Lyneham, Wootton Bassett, Purton & Cricklade libraries. Opening hours were increased from 24 to 37 hours per week. Alterations including the rear extension cost £23,500.

Malmesbury Civic Trust 1997

Gordon Williams
c1977

The combined Primary School opened in 1966 and the layout is shown opposite when there were nearly 450 pupils. The wooden classroom nearest the road above had been built in 1948. The Grammar School in 1953 had added a long brick building the end of which is shown below right together with three temporary classrooms. Joseph Poole's 1883 building (later the Cartmell Centre) for preparing his myriorama paintings was also used for classes. In the centre the corrugated iron porch erected after stones fell from the building in January 1981.

Malmesbury Primary School 1982

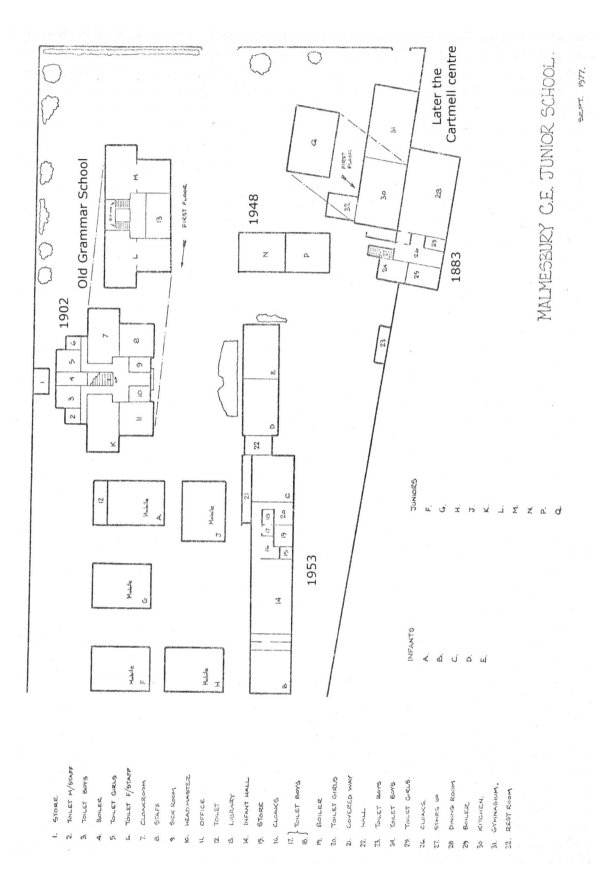

MALMESBURY C.E. JUNIOR SCHOOL.

SEPT. 1977.

Old Grammar School

1902

1948

1953

Later the Cartmell centre

1883

FIRST FLOOR

FIRST FLOOR

1. STORE.
2. TOILET M/STAFF
3. TOILET BOYS
4. BOILER
5. TOILET GIRLS
6. TOILET F/STAFF
7. CLOAKROOM
8. STAFF
9. SICK ROOM
10. HEADMASTER
11. OFFICE
12. TOILET
13. LIBRARY
14. INFANT HALL
15. STORE
16. CLOAKS
17. TOILET BOYS
18. TOILET BOYS
19. BOILER
20. TOILET GIRLS
21. COVERED WAY
22. HALL
23. TOILET BOYS
24. TOILET BOYS
25. TOILET GIRLS.
26. CLOAKS.
27. STAIRS UP
28. DINING ROOM
29. BOILER.
30. KITCHEN.
31. GYMNASIUM.
32. REST ROOM

INFANTS
A.
B.
C.
D.
E.

JUNIORS
F.
G.
H.
J.
K.
L.
M.
N.
P.
Q.

29

Malmesbury Primary School 1982

Above 14 July 1982. Extensions to the brick building have begun. Three portakabin classrooms in the foreground. Part of the grounds to the north were sold for an extension to the cemetery. Below 7 October 1982. One portakabin was removed to create space for the east extension. The exterior of the new building is nearing completion. To help pay for the £444,000 work, land was sold for a house on Tetbury Hill.

Malmesbury Primary School 1982

Malmesbury Primary School 1983

The oldest and youngest pupils, Elaine Trimble and Helen Ringer, perform the opening ceremony on 31 January 1983. The new building contained eight classrooms and the roll totalled 285 at the time. On site there was a fully equipped gymnasium, a music room and a special toilet and shower for the disabled. In April the old school was demolished to make way for a carpark and turning space for school buses.

Malmesbury Primary School 1983

Malmesbury Civic Trust
c1920

The Technical School, opened in 1896 for five pupils behind the Council Chamber in Silver Street, proved so popular that new premises to accommodate 75 were built on Tetbury Hill in 1903. The Gazette described it: *On the left of the central entrance is a room for the caretaker, and on the right is the principal's room. Right and left are classrooms, for boys and girls respectively, and the cookery and manual instruction rooms - separate entrances and cloak-room accommodation being provided. On the portion of the first floor above the boys' department are provided physical and chemical laboratories; over the main entrance ... the lecture room is placed; .. an additional class-room and the art room - these last two arranged that by the removal of a partition can be made into one large room. The building will be made of stone from the Garsdon quarries and the roof with green slates.* Below Verona House built by Joseph Poole in 1883 was bought for the Headmaster in 1921.

Malmesbury Civic Trust 1964

Malmesbury Civic Trust 1999

Although the Malmesbury and District Secondary School was taken over by Wiltshire County Council shortly after it moved into the new premises, parents still had to pay for their children's education. In the 1930s fees were three, six, nine or twelve guineas a year according to their income and financial responsibilities. With increased numbers a new building was put up on 11 acres at Filands in 1964. This had nine classrooms, rooms for chemistry, physics, biology and art, sixth form accommodation and a 'magnificent' library. The assembly hall could accommodate the whole school which started out with 370 pupils. In 1971 under the new Comprehensive system both secondary schools combined and Filands became the Lower School. In 2001 a new larger building opened at Corn Gastons and Filands was sold.

Malmesbury Civic Trust 2002

Malmesbury Civic Trust 1964

Finally (under the Education Act 1944) in 1954 the Malmesbury Secondary Modern School was built on land at Corn Gastons the County Council had bought prior to the war. In 1964 there were 623 pupils and the teachers had a interesting car collection including a 10 year old Morris Oxford, a Minivan and a Morris Minor. The view below shows the area where school buses came in from Bremilham Road, dropped off or picked up and exited along Pool Gastons Road. To the west of the buildings was a large playing field on which the new Malmesbury School now stands.

Malmesbury Civic Trust 1999

After the secondary schools combined in 1971 the logistics of running two separate sites was difficult and expensive. Approval was given in 1998 for a new school to be built at Corn Gastons using the Private Finance Initiative whereby a contractor would construct and run the building for 35 years with rent paid to them. Completed in 2001, Malmesbury School has established the Avon Teaching School Alliance and the Athelstan Trust to share its expertise with other schools.

Below - the Church of England Primary School moved into a new building in June 2008. This is further from Tetbury Hill and 38 houses have been built in Poole Road on the old site.

Malmesbury Civic Trust 2020

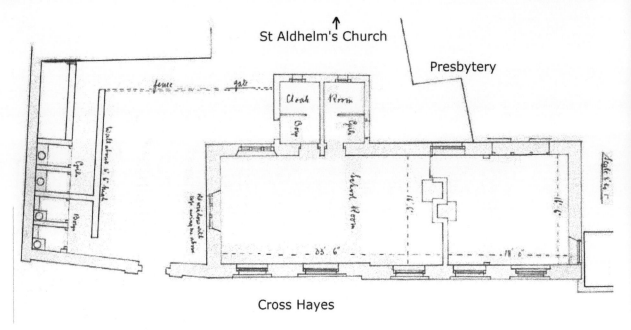

St Aldhelm's Church

Presbytery

Cross Hayes

Father Larive, the first Roman Catholic priest, started what would now be called adult literacy classes in 1867. This led his parishioners asking him to run a free Elementary School, which opened in two rooms of Cross Hayes House the next year called St Joseph's. When the new church was built the school moved into the old building, floor plan above. As the school was free it proved very popular and the Nonconformists sought to persuade parents to remove their children. As a result they opened the Ragged School, but St Joseph's flourished. The Sisters of Mercy taught, using Cross Hayes House as a convent 1870-1884.

Malmesbury Chronicles 1985

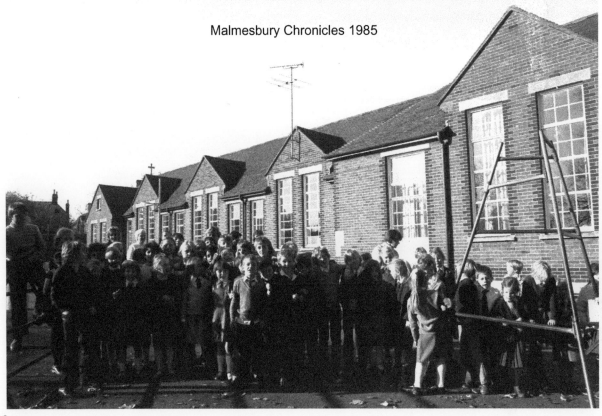

In 1930/1 St Joseph's moved to a new building in Holloway, on the left below and above. That building is still in use but the area where the pupils stood in 1985 is now occupied by a flat roofed extension shown above. Teachers from the Order of St Joseph of Annecy used the Nuns Walk below the town wall until 1990 when their convent closed at Cross Hayes House.

Unfortunately no photo has been found of the Ragged School so an 1889 map is used. A wooden building donated by Walter Powell MP was erected on land in Burnivale where there are now garages. This free school was opened in 1870. It was difficult to raise funds to meet the expenses and the school closed in 1886.

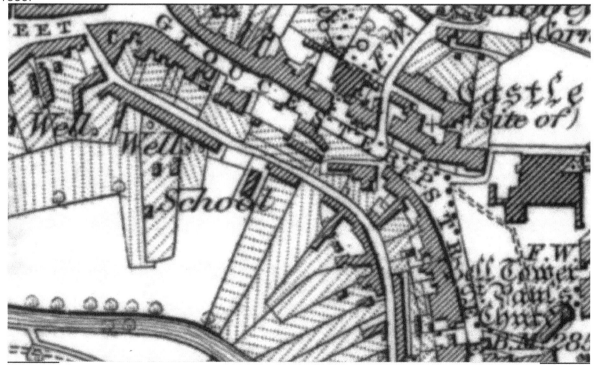

Bob Browning
c1900

Mrs Julia Clark took over a school for young ladies begun by Ellen & Emily Gardner and by 1893 had moved it to Stainsbridge House, above. After Mrs Clark's death one of her assistants, Geraldine Elder, continued until she had to return home to look after her sick father in 1930. Below the classroom of the Athelstan School, Ingram Street. In 1940 Mrs Ellen Hawxwell who had been forced to leave St Joseph's on her marriage, was persuaded to open her own school. In 1952 it moved to Ingram Street. She retired in 1976 and the school closed five years later.

Liz Snell
c1960

Burton Hill House, designed by renowned architect Charles Cockerell, was built in 1846. It was a private residence until leased by Misses 'Zoo' and Hilary Hunt in 1936 as a nursery school. They established an excellent reputation, the school was successful until 'Zoo' died and it closed in 1945. The following year the Shaftesbury Society bought the estate. On 19 July 1947 the Residential School for Seriously Crippled Girls was officially opened. There was accommodation for 50 pupils and from 1961 boys were admitted. Facilities were improved - 1964 a hydrotheraphy pool opened, 1977 an extension with two classrooms called the Brocklebank Wing and 1987 a Field Studies Centre to attract groups from other schools to study local history, geography and the environment. The drive to integrate handicapped children into mainstream education led to closure in 2007. Fortunately most of the interior features had been preserved and after several false starts it is now a luxury home.

Malmesbury Civic Trust 1964

Sue White
c1935

Westhill House, Bristol Street, was bought by Isaac Beak, a retired farmer, shortly after the First World War. In the 1920s his son Ronald started a forage merchant's in the house stable block to the west but after his marriage moved home to No 51. Two of his sisters, Gertrude & Eileen, opened a Parents' National Education Union school around 1933. It seems to have been a preparatory school to equip children for the Malmesbury Secondary School. Possibly it appealed to non-Conformist families not wanting to use either the Church of England or Roman Catholic Schools. After Ronald died in 1937 his widow moved into Westhill Isaac's widow and her two daughters moved to Cirencester in 1939 so the school closed.

Sue White
c1935

Bob Browning
c1990

In 1908 Ellen Sharpe sold the family's boot & shoe shop at 14 High Street and moved to High View House, 53 Foundry Road with two of her daughters. Evelyn, the eldest, was a music teacher and many of her pupils passed the Associated Board of the Royal Academy of Music & Royal College of Music examinations. The younger sister, Ellen, had been an Elementary School teacher but after her marriage to Arthur May became a voice projection and singing teacher. Thus the High View School of Music was formed. Dorothy Morris joined as a pupil in the late 1930s and after gaining her qualification became a teacher in 1951. At some stage an old hut (pictured above) was re-erected in the drive and used for piano tuition. Evelyn died in 1957 and it is believed Dorothy stopped teaching in the 1960s. The hut is now the waiting room at Blunsdon on the Swindon-Cricklade Heritage Railway (below).

Swindon & Cricklade Railway 2019

Emergency Services & Healthcare

Malmesbury Civic Trust 2020

Wiltshire was the first county to establish a Police force, reflected in their motto *Primus et Optimus* - First and Best. Founded in 1839 officers were based in Malmesbury within a year but it was not until 1853 that the first Police Station was built in Horse Fair, now Burnham Road, pictured above. It comprised three houses, the larger one on the right for the Sergeant and station with two smaller houses for Constables. Behind the station was a cell block, the roof line of which can still be seen from the car park. There was a stable block at the back of the yard shown below and above right. Malmesbury was one of nine Divisions in the county supporting 10 village stations (usually the house where a Constable lived), manned by a Superintendent, three Sergeants and 11 Constables.

Malmesbury Civic Trust
c1900

There was at first some local opposition, but soon the new facility was welcomed. Above the Superintendent in his four-wheel cart, costing £32, in the early 20th Century. The new station at Burton Hill opened in 1955 and the old premises were sold. The yard has been turned into a car park. The cell extension and stables which had been in the corner were demolished. Below a large house by the road and others behind were built but have now been sold. The station (in the centre) is expected to close soon having been busy during the summer of 2020 whilst Royal Wootton Bassett's station was being rebuilt to accommodate Wiltshire North's Community Police Teams..

Malmesbury Civic Trust c1904

On Friday 30 July 1852 there was a fire in straw ricks by the river. Many people rushed to help and Richard Blackford, Kings Arms publican, climbed on top to direct their efforts. Unfortunately he fell into the fire and died in agony the following day. The fire engine (left) was within 10 yards of the river and two yards from the fire but was *"obliged frequently to stop for want of water... the stream of water thrown by the thing is so small, that a common garden syringe would be as efficient."* This appliance had also failed at the major fire which destroyed Burton Hill House in 1846.

A committee was formed to raise £150 to buy a new fire engine. Insurers, businesses and prominent local people all contributed. The engine was delivered in May 1853 and the committee organised the brigade. It consisted of a staff of 12 with the Shand & Mason fire engine. There was eighty feet of hose for which water would be drawn from local wells and rivers. The Brigade consisted of a superintendent, officers, firemen, and hosemen. Anyone who had subscribed 10s. or more did not pay charges for attendance at fires.

Below the new and old engines.

Malmesbury Civic Trust c1905

In 1868 responsibility passed to the Vestries of the Abbey (1/40th), St Paul (29/40ths) & Westport (10/40ths) and the engine was kept in the Tolsey Gate - note the double doors.

The new Borough Council took over in 1886. The Fire Station moved from the Tolsey to the Hurdle Store, Cross Hayes in 1887. There were fixed charges for the services given by the Brigade. In 1901 the brigade was in poor shape: *engine, couplings, hose ... hydrants in a very defective state ... the Brigade lacking in discipline and drill ...* It was decided to disband and reform it. The reformed Brigade consisted of: Superintendent, Engineer, Foreman, and 7 Firemen. The Engineer was paid £2 for the upkeep of the engine. All members were insured with the London Guarantee and Accident Company. The Brigade introduced rules including: *"Immediately upon the hearing the ringing of the bell it will be the duty ... to attend the fire station."*

In 1910 an appeal raised £412 from the public, sufficient to buy a Merryweather Greenwich Gem steam pump (named Alexandra after the newly widowed Queen) and half a mile of hose (right). The appliance could pump 300 gallons a minute but took 10 minutes to raise steam. The old appliance was kept as the *... new fangled modern appliance was not completely reliable and ... the manual was of a more practical ability.* Regulations stipulated the new engine was to have a minimum crew of four men. With it weighing 2 tons 2 cwt (with a man on board) proper horse power was essential. Harry Jones provided horses, hired at £2 2s. per day within a five mile radius. Later Lord Suffolk presented two horses to the Brigade.

Athelstan Museum
c1900

Athelstan Museum
c1910

Athelstan Museum
1925

In the 1920s Councillor E. M. Scott Mackirdy was chairman of the committee becoming the driving force behind the Brigade. Captain Bowman retired after being in charge for some twenty years and Lt. 'Eggy' Edwards replaced him. The Town Council bought the Town Hall in 1921 and the following year the Brigade moved there. After much discussion and controversy the steam pump was put up for sale and money collected to buy a motor driven fire engine. An example took part in the Hospital carnival (left).

In October 1925 the 250-300 gallon Dennis 35 hp fire engine with ladder, christened "King Athelstan" was delivered. It had spoked wheels and solid tyres. It was said *... since 1921 we have scrapped all our fire junk including the fire station and no vehicle in commission today was on the inventory four years ago.* £1060 was needed but only £800 raised so the Council borrowed the balance – this was collected by October 1926. Below Herbert Storey is shown presenting the cheque with Mrs Mackirdy on the right about to unveil a brass plaque, now kept in the Gloucester Road Fire Station. This was the last appliance to be bought by public subscription.

Malmesbury Civic Trust
1925

MR 5084

Bob Browning
1925

After the handover of the new engine on Sunday 25 October 1925 it and Cirencester's were taken to the Silk Mills to be put through their paces.

Below the Brigade at Maidford, Norton.

Gordon Williams
c1930

BOROUGH of MALMESBURY
FIRE BRIGADE

Malmesbury Civic Trust
1926

In the early hours of 24 March 1926 a fire started in the nursery at Sopworth House. The local Postmaster telephoned for help but was unable to contact the Malmesbury exchange because the operator was asleep. By the time the town's engine got there the Chippenham Brigade were present and the fire had such a hold that the building was completely destroyed.

On Sunday 20 November 1927 Capt E. M. S. Mackirdy entertained the Councillors in the Town Hall to celebrate his third term as Mayor. Outside was a Studebaker ambulance which he presented to the Fire Brigade. In 1931 this vehicle broke down and was replaced by a Buick.

Malmesbury Civic Trust
1927

Athelstan Museum
1939

In preparation for war, the Auxiliary Fire Service was formed. In May 1939 two Coventry Climax trailer pumps were ordered for Malmesbury, one of which is shown above with John Westmacott, Dennis Poole, Claud Gale, Francis 'Fessor' Wood, Fire Chief Egbert Edwards, Arthur Rogers, Jack Thornbury, David Adye, Percy Poole, Oswald Jones with Frank Weston in the background.

The National Fire Service was formed in November 1941 and took over the Brigade's men and equipment. On Monday 13 March 1944 a serious fire occurred at Linolite's factory in the Postern Mill. Unfortunately the town's King Athelstan appliance failed to start but five pumps employing eight jets fought the blaze which had a firm hold before the alarm was raised. The Town Council called for a report from the NFS after which they concluded that the town was better protected than it had ever been.

Malmesbury Civic Trust 1964

Athelstan Museum
1952

In September 1946 the Town Council decided to scrap the 21 year old Dennis appliance which was replaced by an Austin towing a trailer pump. In April 1948 the NFS disbanded and Wiltshire County Council took over. An Austin K2 Hose Reel Tender, registration GXH 372, with a Dennis trailer pump was delivered in September 1952 and this combination was to remain until 1964. It is shown above with (from the left): Bob Davisson, Harvey Frayling, Cyril Ponting, John Westmacott, George Bartlett, Vincent Edwards, Herbert Paginton, Dennis Poole, Bert Avis, Charlie James, Victor Peters & Percy Lewis.

The pump is shown below on the left. Harvey Frayling (below) joined the Fire Brigade whilst employed at Ekco early in the war. He retired in 1972 after serving as Station Officer for 27 years.

Malmesbury Civic Trust
1952

Lynette Babidge
1962

The narrowness of the Town Hall exit caused problems as appliances got bigger to carry more equipment. In 1964 a narrow Dennis F8 built in 1953 was transferred from Calne. This remained until a new station was built.

The Borough Council bought the eight acre site of the former railway station in 1966. The County Council bought one acre nearest Gloucester Road and the first development was the Fire Station, opened in August 1969.

Terry Thomas c1965

Malmesbury Civic Trust 2020

Chris Harvey
1979

The old fire pump, retired when the Malmesbury Brigade was formed, was repaired by the local crew. Here it is handed over by Station Officer Bill Sharpe to Mayor Peter Curtis on behalf of Athelstan Museum.

In December 1979 Malmesbury took delivery of the County's first Dodge appliance. It had a V8 diesel engine with the latest rescue equipment including a new type of hook-on roof ladder, cutting gear and a high pressure pump to produce a 'fog' spray to reduce water damage.

Malmesbury Chronicles 1985

Above the Dennis' hook-on ladder is put to good use at a chimney fire in Parklands.

Below - seeking to recruit new part-timers at the Market Cross, 10th July 1999. The personnel are Fire Fighter Risby, Sub Officers Snell and Newman (in charge of the station) with Fire Fighters Thomas and Jones. At the time there were 11 on strength, including one woman. The appliance was one of the first Dennis Sabres, designed by a consortium of five brigades, with an exhaust brake, winch, cutting and lifting gear.

Malmesbury Civic Trust 1999

Malmesbury Fire Station – May 2004

Chris Harvey
2004

Back Row: Ff Terry Fearfield, Ff Andy Mills, Ff Paul Wright, Ff Steve Mills
Middle Row: Ff Juliet Lewin, Ff Nik Daines, Ff Chris Harvey, Ff Chris Thomas
Front Row: Ff Roy Evans, LFf Rob Denley, SubO Wayne Jones, T/LFf Ollie Smith, Ff Andy Waller

The Brigade has to deal with many emergencies in addition to fires including motor accidents, and floods. On 23 April 2007 James Brown returned home and switched on the kettle for a cup of tea. Immediately an explosion destroyed his Horsefair home. It transpired that a contractor renewing gas mains had connected a redundant pipe leading into the house. Remarkably James and his dog survived with minor injuries.

Chris Harvey
2007

Chris Harvey
2013

Above left Malmesbury's Dennis Sabre appliance 2005-2013 and right a Scania P280 delivered new on 23rd April 2013. Below the crew in March 2020: Back row Fire Fighters Alexander Hughes, Tom Sweatman, Neil Risby, Jae Wright, Jack Rees, Tim Burns; Front row Fire Fighter Ryan Smith, Crew Manager Jamie Johnstone, Watch Manager Chris Harvey, Crew Manager Tom Gardiner, Fire Fighter Bret Gardiner. Samantha Smith was missing.

Chris Harvey
2020

Malmesbury Civic Trust 1964

GEORGE HOTEL

Dave Poole
1969

AMBULANCE

JMW 814F

When the National Fire Service was formed the ambulance needed to be removed from the Town Hall to a garage behind the George. This is shown above with Roper's Fish & Chip shop, the rear of Stan Hudson's garage and a wall at the back of E & S's shop. The Fire Brigade's Buick ambulance failed and a Rolls Royce was borrowed for use during the war. In 1946 the Red Cross provided the Borough with an ambulance for £20 pa. The National Health Service Act 1946 passed responsibilty to Wiltshire County Council. A Substation was formed in the town with a driver on call supported by seven volunteers. In 1958 Malmesbury received a new ambulance, the 4 berth Austin Princess is shown on the left outside the Town Hall which was leased after the Fire Brigade left in 1969.

Mark Westmacott
c1980

The garage in the Town Hall was initially leased for five years. In 1974 responsibilty for the service passed from the County Council to Wiltshire Area Health Authority. In July 1978 a purpose built facility, costing £72,000, was opened in Station Yard, next to the Fire Station. After many years of previous poor service it was now much improved thanks to the three ambulances and crews based here. Above are Roger Backway, Alan Jones, Divisional Officer Pat Scully, Terry Soule, Dave Thornbury and Keith Westmacott. Further changes in the controlling authority have taken place - Wiltshire Ambulance Trust in 1996, Great Western Ambulance Trust 2006 and South Western Ambulance Service 2013. Being on the northern fringe of the latter's huge area covering 20% of mainland England with a far smaller percentage of the population, the future of Malmesbury's station is in doubt.

Mark Westmacott
c1980

Caroline Pym
c1867

Tower House was used as a General Practitioner's house and surgery for over 100 years. Above Dr. Alfred Jeston (who died in 1869) and his wife sit on the left with Dr. Kinneir on the right who retired in 1902. Doctors Heaton, Maitland-Govan, O'Connor, Battersby and Winch were their successors. Dr. William Winch came from Southend in 1937 and retired 20 years later when Dr. Michael Pym (below) took over.

Caroline Pym 1964

Bob Browning
c1975

Gloucester House, 10 Gloucester Street, was the main surgery for a group of doctors, supposed to be one of the oldest practices in the country. Dr. Bernulf Hodge joined Drs. Robert Pitt and Reginald Moore (who lived at Mundens, Abbey Row) in 1929. In retirement he is shown above centre in a very un-PC setting. The Tower House surgery moved to Laystalls, Cross Hayes (below) in 1978 where Dr. John Rycroft became the senior partner and was joined by Drs. Babcock and Charles. Meanwhile Dr. Alexander Sillars joined the Gloucester House practice in 1952 and Dr. Barrie Crane in 1968. Their surgery moved to Prospect House, Olivers Lane. As time passed both surgeries needed more space so in 1988 they combined at Gable House, 46 High Street (right).

Malmesbury Chronicles 1985

Nigel Pickering 2010

Nigel Pickering 1990

Above Back row: Janet Pickering, Angie & Dr. David Charles, Dr. Nigel Pickering, Dr. Kate Badcock, David Badcock. Front row: Dr. John & Gill Rycroft.

Left - Doctors Mike Brummitt, Pickering, Badcock, Barrie Crane, Heather Greenwood, Charles and Chris Townsend (who died in a microlight crash in 2005).

Below - the opening of the new Primary Care Centre 21 November 2008 Drs. Badcock & Charles, Prince Charles, Drs. John Pettit, Jackie Neal and John Harrison.

Nigel Pickering 2008

Although the doctors were able to offer good medical treatment for the time, there was no dedicated place for operations or constant nursing supervision. It was not until 1893 that a nursing institute was built by Charles Luce in Cranmore (now Abbeyfield) House, Market Cross. Soon its five beds proved to be inadequate and Colonel Luce provided the Prince and Princess pub and adjacent Reading Room (seen above) to be rebuilt into the Cottage Hospital (below).

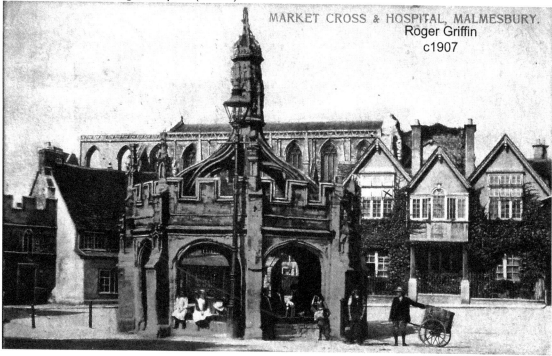

Malmesbury Civic Trust
1925

As described later the hospital expanded during the First World War to cope with the large number of sick and wounded soldiers. One of the buildings used was Burton Hill's Manor House (above). This had been bought by Herbert Storey, a wealthy Lancashire industrialist, who wanted to be near the Beaufort Hunt. In 1925 he moved across the road to Burton Hill House and put the Manor House on the market. It was bought by the Hospital Committee and converted to its new use with 30 beds, five private wards, six maternity beds and an operating theatre. The services offered increased over the years with specialist clinics and X-rays for example. Extra buildings were added including the Minor Surgery unit (below). Senior nurse Bob Sanderson is shown preparing for an endoscopy.

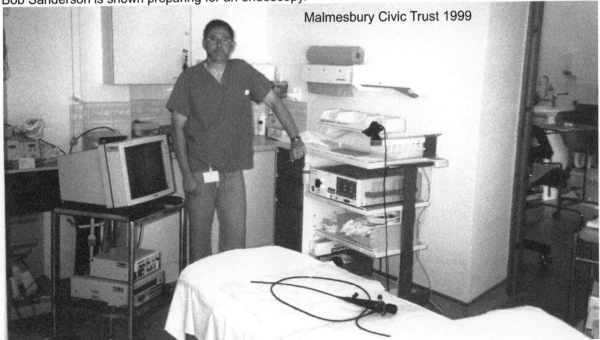

Malmesbury Civic Trust 1999

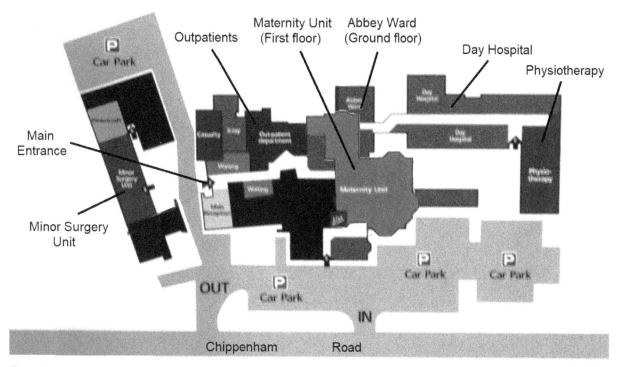

The plan above shows the layout of the site in the 1990s when over 100 babies were delivered, 7,500 casualties treated and 1,500 X-rays taken per year. From this peak services began to be run down. X-rays ended and despite being lauded as a centre of excellence, the maternity unit closed. In 2006 the last patients moved and demolition began. Malmesbury Primary Care Centre (below) contains the town's sole General Practitioners' surgery, an NHS dental practice, Boots Pharmacy, Podiatry and Physiotherapy services. Also on the site is Townsend Court with 28 two-bedroomed flats for the over 55s with a staff member on call, a restaurant and other communal facilities. Next door Athelstan House offers residential, nursing and dementia care for up to 80 residents.

Malmesbury Civic Trust 2020

Military Connections

Malmesbury Civic Trust
c1895

Although the Militia recruited from the town, the first unit to meet and train here was a troop of Wiltshire Yeomanry formed in 1794. They were also used to help keep the peace. Above - the troop on parade outside the Bell Inn and below a group at camp in the summer of 1914.

'Moonraker'
1914

The Malmesbury Bloomers
(Royal Wilts Yeomanry) Pyt. House, Camp, Tisbury,

Members of the Yeomanry troop volunteered for the Boer War. During the Great War they fought as infantry as part of the Wiltshire Regiment from 1917. Between the wars they continued to train as horsed cavalry and were sent to Palestine in 1940 with their horses. There Nigel Carter of Arches Farm, pictured right, died from sand fly fever in 1942. The Regiment took part in putting down the rebellion in Iraq and defeating the Vichy French in Syria before being issued with tanks.

They took part in the battle of El Alamein before returning to Aleppo in Syria for a rest. Our local unit, 3 Troop of C Squadron had Sherman tanks called Malmesbury, Corston and Rodbourne. In 1944 they moved to Italy but at the end of that year the unit disbanded and the Malmesbury troop was not reformed.

David Jones c1936

Royal Wiltshire Yeomanry Association
1943

Athelstan Museum
1901

Malmesbury Civic Trust
1900

Fear of a French invasion in 1859 led to the formation of local rifle volunteers. The 3rd Wiltshire was formed in Malmesbury on 28 January 1860. This became A Company 2nd Volunteer Battalion Wiltshire Regiment in 1888. An officer and 15 men volunteered to serve in the Boer War leaving in January 1900 and returning in April 1901. Unfortunately Lt. Walter Luce and Private Monty Baker from Crudwell (pictured left) died from enteric fever. After arriving by train the whole Company marched to the Town Hall for a ceremony. The parade is shown passing through the Triangle above. A brass memorial was commissioned (shown above right but held in store) and each man was presented with a silver half-hunter watch engraved *Malmesbury's thanks to ...., 2nd V.B. Wiltshire Regiment, for active service in the South African Campaign, 1901.* On the right the unit is shown marching past the Hospital from their drill hall, a wooden building next to the water tower. They were not part of the Territorial Force in 1908.

Malmesbury Civic Trust
2014

Bob Browning
c1904

Malmesbury Civic Trust
c1925

On the formation of the Territorial Force in 1908 it was decided to form 3rd Wessex Brigade Royal Field Artillery's Ammunition Column in Malmesbury. As more than 150 men were required recruits came from a wide area including Tetbury and Swindon as well as the villages. In 1912 a new Drill Hall was built on the Bristol Road to the west of the junction with Bremilham Road, shown above. The Column did not accompany the other units of the Wessex Division which sailed for India in October 1914. In July 1915 the final members of the unit left the town and it was not reformed. Below the Ammunition Column taking part in a military funeral at the Tetbury Hill cemetery, probably Willie Thornbury's. At the end of the war the Drill Hall was sold to Reg Adye who ran his garage from the site until his family sold it in 1982.

Athelstan Museum
c1915

The poor state of British agriculture produced many local recruits for the armed services. At the outbreak of the First World War reservists, including many postmen, were recalled. Old soldiers who had been formed into the National Reserve followed soon afterwards. There was no frantic rush for others to volunteer until the first recruiting meeting on 8th September when 51 young men stepped forward. Many of these were sent to Ireland due to a shortage of recruits there and never returned from Gallipoli. By early 1915 more than 220 men had joined the services from a total population of around 4,000 - perhaps 35% of those of military age. As the war progressed the supply of volunteers ran out and the 'Derby' scheme of late 1915 failed to satisfy the demand so conscription was introduced in April 1916.

After the Territorials, who were intended to provide defence of the homeland, had been dispatched overseas there was still a fear of invasion. In March 1915 a company of the Volunteer Training Corps was formed from men aged under 18 or over 38. Initially without uniform the purpose was to train in the use of rifles and patrol the area. After the introduction of conscription membership became mandatory. Below the Malmesbury Platoon with its commander Lt. F. J. Bates in the centre with Sgt. Maj. W. G. Perry with his dog in front.

Bob Browning
1914

Gordon Williams
1917

John Bowen
1915

The Earl of Suffolk left home to take command of the Swindon Battery of the Royal Field Artillery and the Countess offered the grounds of Charlton Park as a tented camp for Belgian refugees. Then, along with other members of the aristocracy, she turned her home into an Auxiliary Hospital. The Countess provided all of the equipment and the staff came from members of the Malmesbury, Charlton and Crudwell Voluntary Aid Detachments. These VADs were generally middle class women, who probably had domestic servants, given rudimentary nursing training, supported by a few professional nurses. In October 1915 the Countess decided to join her husband in India and the hospital closed, having received 148 patients. The main ward in the picture gallery is shown above and the large number of VADs below.

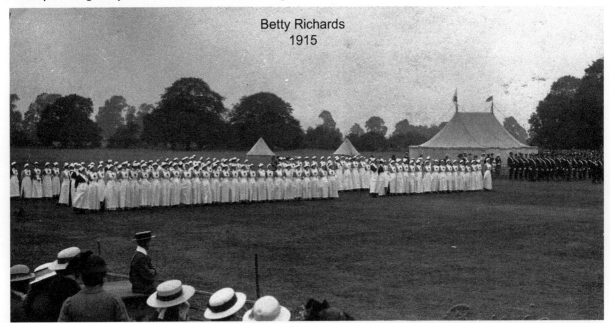

Betty Richards
1915

Jim Rivett
1917

After Charlton Park closed, the local VADs arranged for the Cottage Hospital to register with the Red Cross. When the Battle of the Somme began the Red Cross took charge on 18th July 1916. It required extra capacity and as the Wesleyan Methodist Church had closed for the want of a Minister, this provided an extra ward and a recreation room. The ward, now the Wesleyan Room of the Town Hall, is shown above. Cranmore House (now renamed Abbeyfield House at the Market Cross) and Burton Hill's Manor House later were added so that 100 patients could be accommodated. Gertrude Luce commanded and was awarded the O.B.E. in 1918. The presentation at the Market Cross is shown below. The Red Cross handed control back to the committee in June 1919.

Malmesbury Civic Trust
1918

4th Batt. WILTSHIRE REGIMENT (T.A.)

A Detachment of the above is being formed at Malmesbury. Temporary H.Q. at Wheadon's shop. Prospective recruits are asked to present themselves for enlistment on Tuesday, February 23rd, at 7.30 p.m., and on every subsequent Tuesday, when full particulars will be supplied. Your Country's safety needs YOUR help.

Athelstan Museum
1937

ENLIST NOW !

Preparations for war began in the mid 1930s. In 1937 recruitment for a new platoon of the Wiltshire Regiment's Territorial Army began in Malmesbury led by Bill Wheadon, the hairdresser at 36 High Street. In 1939 when the TA was doubled this unit became part of 5th Battalion. During the same year a new Drill Hall was built on Tetbury Hill now used by the Air Cadets. It has the badges of the Wiltshire Yeomanry and Regiment over the front door. The Yeomanry had previously met behind 32 Cross Hayes.

Malmesbury Civic Trust 2020

72

Malmesbury Civic Trust
1940

Before war was declared 900 school children from Soho arrived on a long train. In accordance with the plan they were taken to the Secondary School to be given food before being disbursed throughout the area. During the 'phoney' war some returned home. However 370 children from Tilbury arrived in June 1940, Shown above two of Val Vernon's aunts are wearing white hats near the centre of the photograph.

As in the previous war the Territorial Army guarded key points in the country. 61 Anti-Tank Regiment came from Arbroath to Malmesbury. Billets were also found in local villages. They departed in April 1940 - picture right. From 1943 9 miles of the Charlton to Minety road became a large vehicle store for 61 Reserve Vehicle Depot.

Malmesbury Civic Trust
1940

73

Malmesbury Civic Trust
c1942

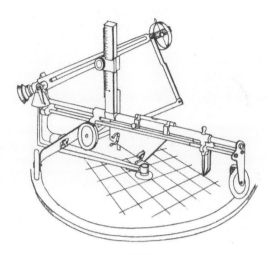

The Observer Corps used the tower of Tower House as Post M1 - two observers were on duty 24 hours a day to keep track of all aircraft movements and report them back to Headquarters at RAF Rudloe Manor near Corsham. Height, direction and speed were calculated using the post instrument above. These men carried out these duties in addition to their civilian jobs. Back row; Alfred Boulton, Ron Pierce, Philip McGoldrick, not known, Frank Weeks. Middle row; Ned Allen, Norman Adye, Stan Weitzel, Walter Barnes, Eric Lightowler, Arthur Phelps, John Mott, Thomas Parks. Front row; Dennis Morse, George Sabey, Stan Hudson, Reg Young, Percy Crowe.

Christine Schofield
1942

After the German blitzkreig which over-ran France, Holland and Belgium in May 1940, invasion was feared at any time and the Home Guard was quickly formed. A battalion was headquartered in town with companies in the villages. They manned check-points and carried out patrols looking for parachutists. The Headquarters team is shown below.

READING FROM LEFT TO RIGHT

Pte. G. W. Broom   Pte. T. A. Paul   Pte. A. E. Player   Pte. A. R. Skinnard   Pte. K. W. F. Steward   Pte. F. Willis   Pte. J. Rich
Pte. J. Clark   Pte. H. Vizor   Pte. H. T. Rooney   Pte. W. A. Pitman   Pte. J. H. Walker   Pte. G. E. Whale   Pte. H. M. Richards   L/Cpl. A. Tidmarsh
Pte. G. Bamfield   Pte. A. R. Toreau   Cpl. B. D. O'Connor   L/Cpl. R. W. Gale   Cpl. E. J. Ratcliffe   Pte. B. H. Clark   Pte. F. W. Mitchell   Pte. W. F. Thornbury
Sgt. I. Cole   2/Lieut. C. W. Essex   Lieut. M. C. Ingram   Lieut. N. W. Evans   Lieut. L. Gardiner   R.S.M. Seager   Sgt. W. C. Brastock   Sgt. A. Clark
Sgt. F. Sharp   Sgt. A. G. Poole

Gordon Williams c1990

In June 1940 it was decided to embark on the massive construction of defensive works throughout the country. The outer defensive line for Bristol was called Stop Line Green. The Royal Engineers fixed the line to follow the River Avon to Malmesbury then an anti-tank ditch would be dug to the north-west. By 9th August the plan had been reconsidered and work was stopped. However in that short period many structures had been built, many of which still exist. Above is a pillbox at Quobwell and below are anti-tank blocks next to the river at Cowbridge. At Long Newnton the depression left after the ditch was refilled is evident.

Jason Bradley 2019

Filands pillbox

Anti-tank ditch
River defence

Jason Bradley 2019

Reeds Farm
pillbox

Whychurch
pillbox

Railway
station

Holloway
bridge

MALMESBURY

Bowls
club

Cowbridge farm
pillbox

E. K. Cole
factory

Burton Hill
pillbox

Cowbridge

Anti-tank
dragon's teeth

Liz Snell
1943

Liz Snell
1943

Throughout the war there were annual events to raise money for the war effort. The Wings for Victory campaign ran from 15th to 22nd May 1943. A whole variety of entertainment was arranged including three one act plays by Athelstan Players, a ball, a dance, a fete organised by E. K. Cole, boxing and shooting competitions.

The highlight was the parade with a Hurricane fighter-bomber and Horsa glider on display. Firemen are seen dispersing from the parade on the left.

The RAF (right) and Wiltshire Regiment bands were present.

The target of £75,000 was exceeded with a total of £119,303 4s 7d raised. A board at the Market Cross recorded the total.

A bakelite plaque was presented to the town.

Liz Snell
1943

Athelstan Museum
1943

Athelstan Museum
1943

Malmesbury Civic Trust
1925

At the end of the First World War there was discussion over the form of a memorial with a park, hospital beds or buying the Town Hall proposed. The result was a Celtic cross designed by Henry de Bertodano, financed by public subscription and built at the Triangle. The Armistice Service of 1925 is shown above. After the 2nd war a children's playgound at St Aldhelms Mead was decided upon. It was opened by the Mayor, Reg Young shown with Bobbie Vince, in August 1950. The slide was deemed dangerous and closed.

Olive Kemp
1950

Branches of ex-servicemen's organisations were formed here after the Great War. In 1921 these combined into the British Legion. A club was opened at 9 Ingram Street which later moved to the rear of 12 High Street in Cross Hayes. After the next war Sir Richard Luce bought the Social Club in Ingram Street for them. This closed in the 1980s. On the right Parade Marshal John Taylor leads Standard Bearer Dick Taylor and escorts Dennis Mason and Bill Selby.

RAF Hullavington was granted the Freedom of the Borough in April 1970. They regularly exercised this Freedom until 1992 when the Station closed. 9 Regiment Royal Logistic Corps, the new unit at the station, (now renamed Buckley Barracks) were granted the Freedom in June 2010.

Jennie Brock
c1990

Athelstan Museum
1970

Transport

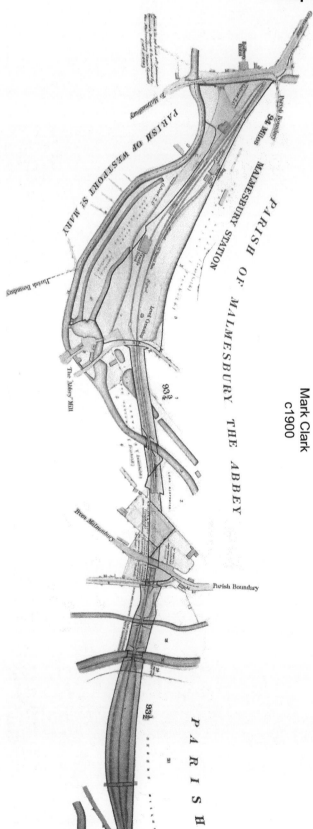

Mark Clark
c1900

Malmesbury's geography has not helped its transport links. The Romans built the Fosse Way 2½ miles to the west of the town and since then major long distance routes such as canals and early railways bypassed the town. However local businessmen saw the benefits of a rail connection so began lobbying for one. Various schemes were considered but it was the Wiltshire and Gloucestershire Railway which looked likely to succeed. Their plan was to connect the Great Western line near Dauntsey to the Midland at Stonehouse or Stroud. A grand ceremony was held in a field near the Duke of York on 1st July 1865 when the Countess of Suffolk turned the first sod with a silver spade, now held in the Athelstan Museum. However a dispute arose over which company would operate the line and the scheme collapsed.

The Malmesbury Railway Company's plan was less ambitious - to connect the town with Dauntsey. Capital was raised, a contractor appointed and work began in July 1874. It involved considerable civil engineering work. The route followed the River Avon resulting in 17 bridges, 3 level crossings, cuttings, embankments and a tunnel under Holloway to reach the station site. Cost overruns led to disputes with the contractor, more capital being called for until in May 1877 the Great Western Railway took full control. They quickly completed the work and the line was opened on 18th December 1877. The branch was shortened by connecting to the South Wales line at Little Somerford in 1933. After the Second World War usage markedly decreased and on 8th September 1951 the last scheduled passenger train was run. Freight continued until 1962 and the track was lifted the following year.

To the left is part of a GWR map originally printed on linen. It must have been prepared before the end of the 19th Century as the ownership details shown date from then but other information is much later.

Athelstan Museum
c1960

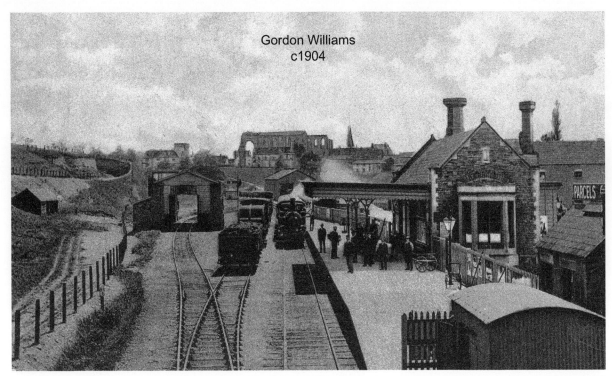

Gordon Williams
c1904

Above the terminus is seen in its heyday. At this time there were 7 trains each way every weekday with one on Sunday. Also a goods train ran on the last Wednesday of the month to bring livestock to and from the town's market. After the passenger service ended freight continued until 1962. The major customer was A. B. Blanch of Crudwell whose agricultural machinery was bulky and more economical to transport by rail. Below the cattle dock is seen on the right which had not been used after the war and the barn to the left rented to a farmer.

Gordon Williams
c1962

Jim Gilmore 1962

The last excursion train was run by the Gloucester Railway Society on 31st July 1962. It comprised a steam Pannier tank engine coupled to two B Set coaches - a combination similar to that which had run the scheduled services before closure.

Below - the track has been lifted and the goods shed demolished. The Engine Shed is now used by Kwik-Fit.

Gordon Williams
c1965

Athelstan Museum
c1880

The photo above shows the entrance to Cowbridge House and its farm with the river bridge on the right. Wiltshire County Council decided to widen this single track bridge in 1929 and that work is shown below. This elegant structure was replaced in 2007 so that 44 tonne vehicles could use the B4042.

Malmesbury Civic Trust
1929

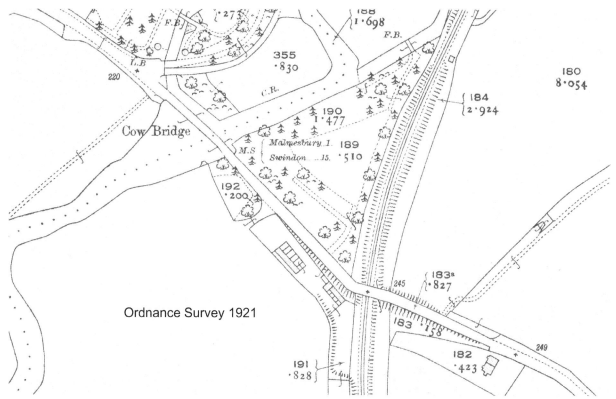

Ordnance Survey 1921

The railway bridge just beyond Cowbridge created a sharp bend in the road which became an accident blackspot. The stone parapet was replaced by railings to improve visibility but the corner remained dangerous. After the closure of the railway the opportunity was taken to create a less severe bend and to reduce the gradient.

Willis Brothers yard occupies the old piggeries shown on the map and part of the track bed south of the bridge, an area originally intended for Cowbridge Halt and later as a loading dock for Ekco.

Paddy Lockstone c1964

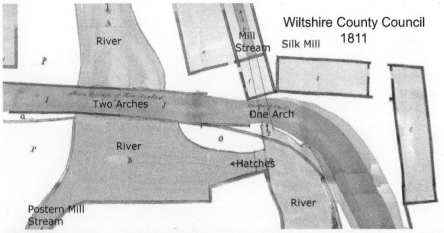

Wiltshire County Council
1811

River

Mill
Stream

Silk Mill

Two Arches

One Arch

River

Hatches

River

Postern Mill
Stream

St John's or the Town Bridge at the bottom of the High Street is the site of an ancient river crossing. There used to be two bridges - a single arch over the mill-stream and two arches over the river as shown on the plan. This was replaced by a culvert to the mill and three arches over the river in 1822. That bridge was widened in 1883 and the hatches shown (left) installed in 1935. The hatches were replaced by 3 weirs in 1979.

Below Holloway Bridge was rebuilt in 1822 as the arches were too small to cope with flood water. Repairs were carried out in 1887. Widening took place in 1935 when the stone arches were replaced by blue bricks.

Bob Browning
c1950

Town Bridge & Almshouses, Malmesbury

Malmesbury Chronicles 1986

Malmesbury Civic Trust
c1960

Staines Bridge was the last bridge to be widened. In 1962 a pre-fabricated concrete span was placed on top of the old bridge which can still be seen from the river path next to the Fire Station. More recently the pavements have been widened and wooden pillars placed in the pavements to prevent two heavy vehicles crossing simultaneously. In the photographs part of Athelstan Garage can be seen on the left, together with an advertising hoarding at the entrance to the livestock market and the Railway Hotel beyond.

Malmesbury Civic Trust
c1970

Malmesbury Civic Trust
1972

Construction of the long anticipated bypass in December 1971. The Priory roundabout is shown above with the old road in the left foreground and the Priory's wall on the right.
The first work by the river is shown below.

Ron Bartholomew
1972

Progress on the bypass bridge is illustrated by the scaffolding used to form the two northern support arches above and below the 20th pre-cast beam being craned onto those arches.

Bob Browning
1925

On 2nd July 1925 Holloway was widened just below the East Gate bastion. As the main route through Malmesbury, the Borough Council were grateful to Henry Garlick who gifted a small strip of land in his will. The afternoon began with the road opening and unveiling of a plaque commemorating Cllr. Garlick. The incongruous scene above occurred because the Secondary School pupils were about to perform an extract from the Athelstan pageant in the Town Hall before the unveiling of stained glass windows in the Assembly Room.

Bob Browning
1925

Opening of the New Roadway at Holloway
At 2.40 p.m. by Mrs. Henry Garlick

Unveiling a Memorial Stone in the New Wall to the Memory of the late Mr. H. Garlick by Alderman H. Farrant, J.P.

In the Town Hall at 3 p.m.

Dramatic Performance by Secondary School Pupils
Under the direction of Miss Kerry, L.L.A.

From

"ATHELSTAN"
A Pageant Play by Miss Kerry and Miss Maby
Episodes III. (part) and VI.

Characters

Athelstan	D. Pike	Archbishop of Canterbury	G. Heath
Adulph	K. Greenfield	Abbot of Malmesbury	F. Curtis
Eadhilda	A. Porter	Hugh of France	R. Player
Harper	N. Clark	Page	G. Marmont
Captain	L. Wood	Eadgitha	J. Ferris
Gurth	C. Eattell	Elfgiva	K. Dinham
	Soldiers	H. Goodfield and D. Baldwin	

Synopsis

Athelstan, finally victorious, is at his Palace at Malmesbury—He arranges his sisters' marriages—Eadhilda's lover, Hugh of France, sends precious and holy gifts to Athelstan by Adulph—Hugh then comes to claim Eadhilda—Athelstan rewards his faithful captains—The harper sings of the Brunanburgh fight, after which the Malmesbury men are rewarded by the gift of Land.

Unveiling of the King Athelstan Memorial Windows
Painted by Mr. Christopher Webb, Guildford

1—"Arms of Malmesbury"
The Gift of the Town   By H. L. Storey, Esq.

2—"King Edward the Elder, reigned 901-924, and who gave Malmesbury its first Charter in 916"
The Gift of the Ex-Mayors   By Joe Moore, Esq.

Thurketyl (named for Athelstan's military commander), otherwise known as Truckle, Turtle or Westport Bridge on Foxley Road was rebuilt in 1930. The latest construction techniques were used - substantial reinforced concrete piers, a concrete stream bed to improve the flow with a reinforced concrete deck containing 13 9" x 7" RSJs. Over the years the steel reinforcement under the deck began to rust away so in 2019 it was rebuilt. It took over 3 months to complete the work as the structure's strength required considerable effort to remove. Each span's concrete was cut into 9 strips, loosened at each end and lifted out by a large crane, shown above. Then 6 new pre-cast strips were lifted in (below), utility pipes and cables reinstalled, the road resurfaced and parapets rebuilt.

Malmesbury Chronicles
c1925

The number of Malmesbury's coaching inns suggests it used to be an important stopping place for travellers between Wiltshire and the Midlands and Oxford to Bristol but no illustrations have been found. The first motor bus service was started by Bristol Tramways linking Malmesbury with Bristol in 1921. Just after this Norton Motor Services, above, ran three services from Cirencester to Malmesbury on Mondays, Wednesdays and Fridays. This continued until the firm was sold to Athelstan Coaches in 1960. Athelstan Coaches was founded in 1947 and constructed a depot in the Park Road old timber yard, below. The houses of Park Mead are now on the site.

Coach Farmer c1947

Athelstan Coaches was formed by Edward Couzens, a Great Somerford builder and Stan Hudson, the High Street motor dealer. In 1948 they were joined by Jack Grimes who became the sole owner in 1954. They mainly ran excursions but in 1950 applied for a licence to run a bus service between Malmesbury and Cirencester which they obtained despite an objection from Nortons. It was not until 1961 that their bus services expanded with routes serving Pool Keynes, Charlton, Oaksey, Hankerton and Crudwell. Other coach companies were taken over in the 1960s - Coopers of Calne, Barnes of Dauntsey, Pendlebury of Oaksey, Norton's, Fry of Braydon, Sherstonian and Cliffords of Brinkworth. Below - their Market Cross office.

Malmesbury Chronicles 1985

Coach Farmer 1974

Most local bus services used to be run by Bristol Tramways (Bristol - Swindon, Chippenham - Malmesbury via Sutton Benger) and Western National (Stroud - Trowbridge). In the 1950s they introduced double-deckers and one is seen above behind one of Athelstan's coaches. The bus stops were in the centre of Cross Hayes between 1956 and 1975. Below a Bristol LS one man operated bus is shown. By 1962 there were three companies which ran 231 buses through the town each day but fares were rising and car ownership increasing. In 1970 all Western National services were transferred to Bristol Omnibus which threatened to remove all services in 1971. Wiltshire County and other Councils began paying subsidies.

Gordon Williams
c1960

Gordon Williams
c1988

By 1980 Bristol was no longer the main operator - Athelstan, Fosseway and Hatts also ran buses before the industry was deregulated in 1985. Tony Nielson took over Athelstan and renamed it Overland & Counties the following year. Its base was moved to Chippenham but ambitious plans failed and the company went into receivership in 1990. Andy James, based at Easton Grey, which had run school buses for some time, then took over most services until 2014. One of their eight Mercedes 30-seaters is shown below. Coachstyle of Nettleton is the present operator.

Malmesbury Civic Trust 1999

MYSELF MAY 1907.

KM 1015

3½ H.P. BROWN. NEW.
THE FIRST PRIVATELY
OWNED MOTOR IN
MALMESBURY. _____

On the left is an intriguing photo found by David Brooks and now owned by Gordon Williams. Brown Brothers Ltd were component suppliers to the motor industry who made motorcycles between 1902 and 1915. Their 3½ H.P. machine was quite advanced for a price of £37. It is not known who the lucky owner was but he must have been a wealthy young man.

It seems the sole motorist was not alone for long. At least two local businesses offered cars for hire. Jones and Son in 1909 bought the old Primitive Methodist Chapel, 46a Bristol Street, as a garage for their fleet, shown below. Montague Jones ran this business but he was killed in 1918 so after the war Stuart Cole took it over. Ratcliffe and Son was the other company.

Malmesbury Chronicles
c1910

Athelstan Museum
1932

In the 1920s farmers complained it was difficult to park on market days. Six years later the Borough Council set out parking places for the first time - Horsefair 12; outside the Bell Hotel 4; Market Cross 11; Cross Hayes 75; and St Johns Street 14. The photo above shows the small number of cars using Cross Hayes in 1932. In the same year provision was made for 16 cars to park there overnight lit by four street lamps. Above bottom left is E.S.T. Cole's new garage building. The Three Horseshoes pub and blacksmiths, adjacent to the Town Hall, made Cross Hayes Lane very narrow. Bought by the Borough Council in 1938, the intention was to widen the road but this was not carried out until 1957.

A two hour limit was introduced for Cross Hayes parking in 1969 and the town's first Traffic Warden was appointed. In 1996 charges were introduced - 25p per hour. Cross Hayes can now accommodate 93 cars and has four spaces for the disabled.

Malmesbury Civic Trust 2002

Gordon Williams
1936

The proliferation of car ownership is illustrated by the photo on the left of Gloucester Street. The occasion was the Boxing Day meet of the Beaufort Hunt in 1936. This photo appeared in the national press.

Waiting in the High Street was limited to just 20 minutes in 1954 but this was increased to one hour in 1971. Before the one way system was introduced in 1962, parking was only permitted on one side of the High Street. A full time Traffic Warden was appointed in 1996 and since 2006 parking enforcement has been the responsibility of Wiltshire Council. No. 14 High Street had been R.S. Fruiterers, closed in 1985. Now A4 Stationers.

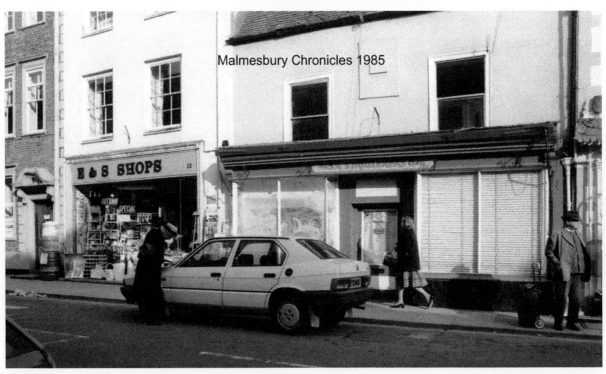

Malmesbury Chronicles 1985

Malmesbury Chronicles 1985

The area around the Market Cross is still a popular place for free parking. When the hospital was in the building now occupied by the Whole Hog, straw was often laid to minimise the noise from traffic. In 1929 it became the first place where vehicles could be parked after dark without lights. Over the years the layout has changed, The 1980s arrangement of spaces next to the carriageway through to Abbey House and against the pavements to the north and west would seem to have allowed the greatest number. Cars are now so large that the present nine spaces leave very little space between. Beyond the van is the Apostle's Spoon Restaurant 1973-1995, later the Rajah Indian Restaurant but closed from 2016 to 2020.

The Station Yard has been used as a car park since 1970, only it was not surfaced with tarmac until 13 years later. Charges were introduced in 2006 and the 145 spaces are now rarely fully occupied. Being next to the river users have sometimes been caught out by floods.

Malmesbury Civic Trust 2000

Old Corporation

Kings Heath, more usually known as the Common, is supposed to have been granted to the men of Malmesbury by King Athelstan as a reward for playing a pivotal role at the Battle of Brunanburh in 927. Athelstan was the first King of all England and particularly favoured Malmesbury, choosing to be buried here.

The wealthy Monastery dominated the town until Dissolution in 1539 but the transfer of power to the Burgesses took many years. By the end of the 16th Century the inner circle of 13 Burgesses annually elected an Alderman. King Charles 1 issued a Charter in 1635 recognising the Corporation (comprising the Alderman, 12 Capital Burgesses, 24 Assistant Burgesses and High Steward as advisor) to be the local government administrators. All these officials had to be freemen or 'commoners' except for the High Steward who was elected annually. There are four grades of freemen - commoner, landholder, Assistant Burgess, Capital Burgess. On admission a commoner's name is added to the 'waiting list' of six subsidiary bodies called hundreds - Taylors, Fishers, Glovers, Coxfoot, Davids Loynes and Thornhill. Each has a membership of 31 landholders and any vacancy is filled by the most senior commoner of that hundred. Vacancies in the ranks of Assistant Burgesses are filled by election of the landholders and among Capital Burgesses by election of the Assistants.

King Athelstan granted five hides or more than 500 acres of land near Norton. After the Enclosure Act 1821 most of it was divided into 280 allotments of about an acre each allocated to a landholder which he could cultivate or rent out. Trustees manage another 50 acres to pay for the maintenance of roads (11 are set out on the common), fences and ditches. The 1829 map on the right sets out the allotments and other lands. Before 1727 any married man living in one of the Borough's ancient tenements could be a commoner. After that date the right was restricted to married sons or sons-in-law of commoners who live within 1½ miles of the Market Cross. At the end of the 20th Century there were insufficient candidates to fill vacancies so from 2000 the qualification on marriage has been lifted and daughters who meet the criteria can join.

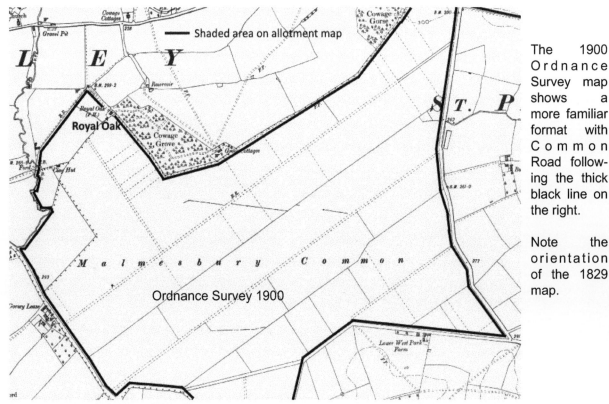

Ordnance Survey 1900

The 1900 Ordnance Survey map shows a more familiar format with Common Road following the thick black line on the right.

Note the orientation of the 1829 map.

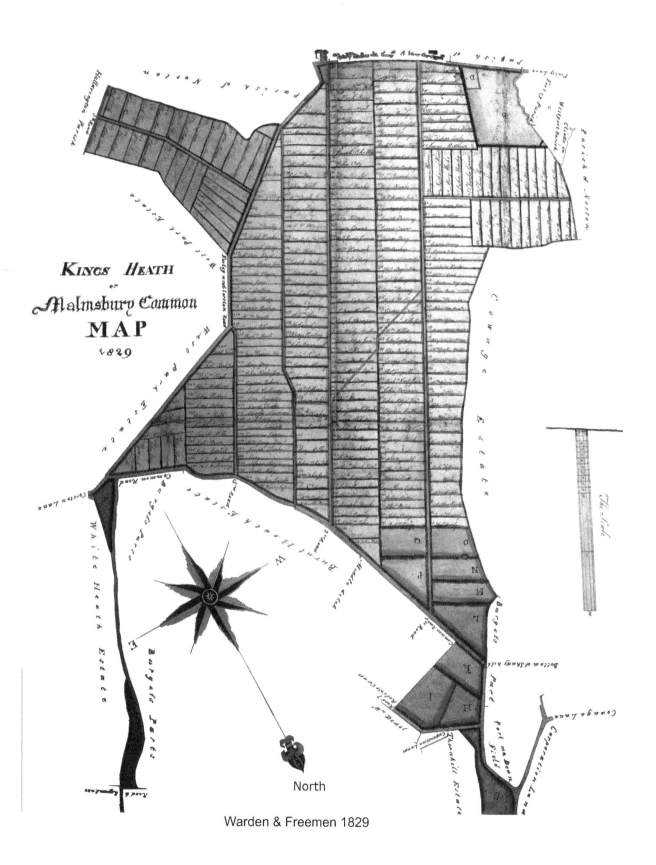

North

Warden & Freemen 1829

Bob Browning
c1925

—FLOGGING THE COMMONERS.—
MALMESBURY.

W.G.SANDY.
MALMESBURY.

New Commoners used to be initiated on New Year's Day at the Common. The initiate would place a silver coin into a hole in the turf and the Surveyor of the Common would recite *Turf and twig I give to thee, the same as King Athelstan gave to me, and I hope a loving brother thou wilt be* whilst striking him three times with a twig. The assemblage would then retire to the Royal Oak (shown on the Ordnance Survey map) which was known as the Slappy. The ceremony now takes place in the Old Court House.

Malmesbury Chronicles 1986

Malmesbury Civic Trust 1964

Around 1590 the Corporation took possession of the Hospital of St John the Baptist in St Johns Street and since 1616 their meetings have taken place in the Court House, above. This building was the magistrates' court from then until 1886 and the Corporation school from 1629 to 1888.

Malmesbury Chronicles 1986

Sarah Cullen
1911

On 9 August 1902 there was a grand celebration of King Edward VII's coronation. Edgar Basevi photographed the Old Corporation's contingent on a platform outside the malthouse at the top of Cross Hayes (now part of the Town Hall).

Left to right: rear, Messrs Wall, Box, Bishop, Russell, Grant & Jefferies; centre Masters Box; front, Messrs Bolton, Pike, Adye, Price, Grant & Chappell.

The Old Corporation owns a number of properties throughout the town including The Guildhall in Oxford Street (now an Italian restaurant) and cottages in Bristol Street. They can be identified by a green plaque. Below - the almhouses in St Johns Street just before they were refurbished. The archway dates back to the 12th Century and was part of the original chapel.

Malmesbury Civic Trust 1964

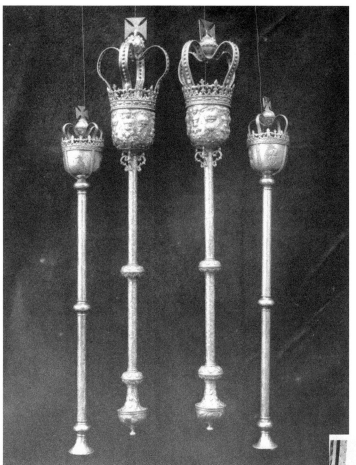

The Old Corporation's maces.

The smaller pair bear the arms of King Charles 1. They probably date from 1635, but have no marks nor inscriptions. They are silver-gilt, 28" in length and weigh 1lb. 6oz. each. The seal of the Corporation of Malmesbury, granted in 1615, is at the end of each mace.

The larger pair bear the arms of Queen Anne, under the crown. One is inscribed on the base *The gift of Thomas Boucher Esq. to the Corporation of Malmesbury anno 1703.* The other *The gift of Edward Pauncefoot Esq. to the Corporation of Malmesbury 1703.* Each weigh 3lb. and are 33" in length. Again the seal of the Corporation is on the end. These were made by Garthorne of London and are silver-gilt.

The Old Corporation sponsored the 1798 *Act for Paving the Footways, and for Cleansing, Lighting, and Regulating the Streets, and other public passages and places within the Borough of Malmesbury, in the County of Wiltshire; and the Avenues leading into the same; and for Removing and Preventing Nuisances, Annoyances and Obstructions therein.* 26 named individuals were appointed Improvement Commissioners who set about improving the public health of the town. They encouraged the formation of the Malmesbury Gas and Coke Company in 1836 which opened gasworks next to the Courthouse, - now a car park. Coal gas was produced there until 1949 when it was piped from Stroud into the gasometers. Gas was used for domestic lighting and supplied all the street lamps up to 1960. After the introduction of natural gas the gasometers were demolished.

This initiative was the main reason why the Old Corporation maintained its political power until 1886, although by then most government functions were carried out by other bodies.

Malmesbury Civic Trust 1964

Business

Malmesbury Market.

Liz Snell
c1925

Agriculture has always been an important element of the local economy with an emphasis on animal hus-
bandry as the soil is best suited for pasture. Markets were held here from medieval times both in the town
centre and in Westport - Horsefair and Sheepfair (the Triangle). Livestock markets were revitalised with
the opening of the railway. They were held on the last Wednesday of the month in Cross Hayes, above.
Below - In April 1950 it moved to the Railway Hotel meadow, Gloucester Road.

Bob Browning
c1955

The meadow was bought by the Borough Council from the Stroud Brewery Company which owned the Railway Hotel. The market was leased to Fielder, Jones & Taylor and Tilley & Culverwell, auctioneers. When meat rationing ended the trade declined and at the end of 1956 several months passed without a market. The leases were terminated and Howes, Luce, Williams & Pane of Chipping Sodbury were appointed, who opened an office at 63 High Street. Trade revived but in 1969 the Meat and Livestock Commission announced the withdrawal of grading facilities which resulted in the market's closure.

Below left is a view looking to the south. Above - the entrance from Gloucester Road and below a view to the north with the old Grammar School in the background.

Malmesbury Chronicles 1985

X-ograph Ltd bought the post war market area from the Town Council in 1982 and built their office and works there (above). They moved to larger premises and from 2000 the building was vacant. Eight years later, Wiltshire Council leased the building and made it into a youth centre since the Cartmell Centre next to the Primary School had been sold for development, A skate park, a facility which had been desired for many years, was built at the rear, Unfortunately funding cuts led to the centre's closure in 2014. Two years later it was turned into Riverside Community Centre and the skate park re-opened (below). At the end of the lane the Boxing Club's gym and the football field's floodlights can be seen.

Malmesbury Civic Trust 2020

John Ponting, who built up a substantial business cen-
tred around 44-46 High Street, opened a builders yard
in Park Road next to the river about 100 yards from the
junction with Gloucester Road (above). His eldest son
Henry was given this part of the business as a wed-
ding present in 1905. Unfortunately he died in 1914 at
the age of 45. His widow, Maude, kept the business
going until in March 1918 she sold the site to Wiltshire
Farmers Ltd. They opened a milk factory the following
year. The company had been set up as a co-operative
for small farmers. The intention was to get the best
price by selling milk to London retailers so it was sent
there in churns by rail. The depot could handle 5,000
gallons per day. On arrival the milk was weighed and
piped to either the cheese making room or the pas-
teurising platform for processing. Finished products
could be stored in a refrigerated room, the door to
which is shown right. In 1923 the company went into
liquidation and Wiltshire Creameries took over. They
amalgamated with United Dairies in 1938 and the factory closed. In 1941 the premises were bought by the
Borough Council which wanted a more reliable water
supply from the spring on site. The premises were allowed to deteriorate until 1968 when North Wiltshire
District Council created a small industrial estate.

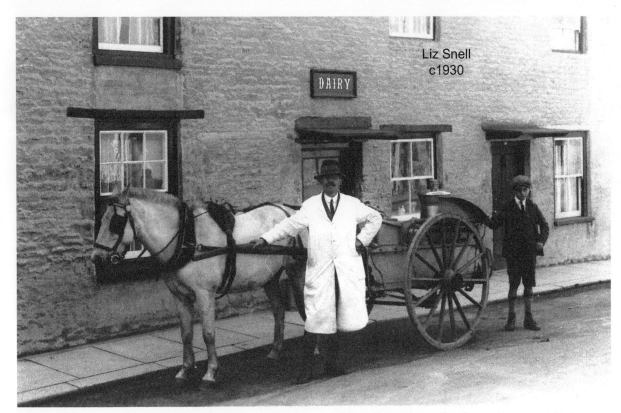

There were a number of milk retailers in town, often selling direct from the farm. Westport Dairy was started in the 1880s - Benjamin Odeland at 6 Bristol Street farmed 40 acres and his neighbour William Young sold the milk. By 1911 Benjamin was the dairyman. Maurice Jefferies (shown above outside No 6) took over around 1930 but closed five years later.

Below the end terrace wall was constructed of Bradstone in 1974 when No 4 was demolished to widen the junction.

BURNIVALE
LEADING TO
THE MALTINGS

Malmesbury Civic Trust 1964

Gastons Dairy seems to have been started by Frederick Bailey at 28 Burnham Road in the 1930s. He kept cows on the field now occupied by the Secondary School. The premises are shown above viewed from Gastons Road. The building on the right, part obscured by a tree, was used for bottling. In 1980 the site was redeveloped and three houses built which are shown below. No 28 is detached on the right, No 30 and No 30a are semi-detached of differing styles.

Malmesbury Civic Trust 2020

Reginald & Gene Kesper bought Gastons Dairy from Frederick Bailey around 1957. They obtained the milk from 3 farms but were prosecuted for selling Channel Island milk ('gold top' costing ½d. extra) with too little fat content. This seems to have been the 'final straw' for selling the business to Will & Marjorie Davies in October 1958. Paul Davies is shown above with the Bedford milk float. Below - Will is on the far left, elder daughter Anthea in front of him with Marjorie next to her, other daughter Corinne in the centre and Paul at the front. The dairy building is on the right with churns outside. A number of men made two deliveries per day, the first beginning at 5am and the second at lunchtime.

Corinne Ratcliffe
c1958

Anthea, Paul & Corinne outside the dairy building. The bottles were hand washed and then sterilised using hot water and caustic soda. Milk was poured into the bottling machine at head height, two bottles (pint, ½ or ⅓ pint but both the same) placed on the left and filled whilst two more were put on the right. Once filled the bottles went into a crate which held 20. The next step was capping with a manual machine using coloured aluminium foil to designate the type of milk. The crates were then stored in a large fridge until needed. At this time only unpasteurised milk was supplied. In 1959 Gastons Dairy took over the rounds of Cowbridge Farm seen below. An electric milk float and roundsmen came with this deal. Extra territory resulted from taking over Dauntsey Vale Dairy which included newspaper deliveries. Later pasteurised milk was delivered by tanker from Stroud Creamery until they were supplying it already bottled. The Dairy closed in 1979 and the site sold for housing.

Malmesbury Chronicles 1986

David Willis c1949

George Moore, a cattle dealer took over the Bell Inn in 1854. It seems he then started a forage business to accompany the stabling at the Inn. His son, Joe, inherited the business and added more stables at Stainsbridge Mill. After Joe Moore sold the Bell, Jack Willis (who had been a partner with his brothers in a similar business in Sherborne) in 1936 took over Stainsbridge and the forage yard at the junction of Park Road. The enterprise supplied animal feed, fertilisers and seed corn. During the war flour was stored in the mill and delivered to local bakers. Later they were one of the first pickup baling contractors. Above - a Vulcan lorry driven by Clive Ponting loaded with potatoes which had been delivered by rail. Note the petrol pump on Gloucester Road near the Park Road junction used to refuel their vehicles. Below - Leyland, Austin and Dodge lorries loaded with hay in the forage yard. In 1958 Rawlings & Phillips bought the business.

David Willis c1953

A plan of the forage yard (right) used for parking vehicles, storing hay plus some pig fattening pens. It was sold to Athelstan Coaches in 1958 and became Athelstan Garage (above after closure). Note they seem to have used the two sheds as their office and showroom. Below - Stainsbridge Mill. The first of the light coloured buildings on the left was used by Mrs Hawxwell for Athelstan School in the 1940s, the other was occupied by Grant Barnes in the 1950s when he started his saddlery business. Rawlings & Phillips owned the site until 1973 when Roy Waine opened Freezer Wise there.

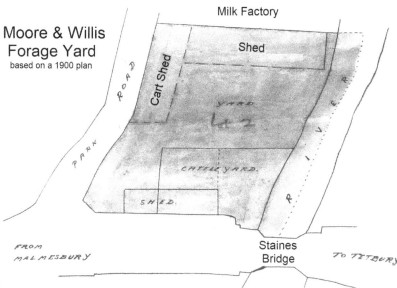

Moore & Willis Forage Yard
based on a 1900 plan

Milk Factory

Shed

Cart Shed

ROAD

PARK

YARD

CATTLE YARD.

RIVER

SHED.

FROM MALMESBURY

Staines Bridge

TO TETBURY.

Malmesbury Civic Trust 1964

Athelstan Museum
c1900

Thomas Edwards and his son John moved their coachbuilding business to Holloway in 1870. John's son Egbert, known as Eggy, joined in 1903 and carried on until his death in 1945 when it was sold to Samuel Hoskins for his son Michael. In 1948 he opened shops including one at 12 High Street still owned by the family. The original workshop is above (now Abbots Gardens) with a mobile display below.

Liz Snell
c1910

ATHELSTAN

John Mott senior brought a travelling cinema to Malmesbury in 1927 which was established in the yard behind the old Unicorn Inn in Lower High Street. This proved popular and in the same year he proposed to build a corrugated iron structure behind the hospital and close to the Abbey. There was fierce opposition to this and it was not until 1934 that permission for a brick building was granted (above). In 1980 it became a Bingo Hall which closed in 1990. St Michael's Court (being built below) occupies the site.

David Shelley
1948

The newly nationalised Southern Electricity Board were anxious to improve the town's electricity supply. In 1948 they opened a new sub-station (above) at the junction of Corn Gastons and Bristol Road. Back row: G. Ferris, E. Ferris, O. Knight, T. Lamb, F. Thomas, A. White, R. Fry, R. Grey, A. Laing-Pearson. Middle row: R. Bilham, R. Dommett, K. Diment, C. Rich, F. Smith, U. Grant, C. Hinder, G. Lockstone, L. Freeman, B. Fry. Front row: M. Cooke, H. Saunders, G. Houghton, W. Ferris, H. Rose, H. Blanchard, J. Shill, M. Hayes, P. Shelley, M. Harris. Mains electricity arrived here with the establishment of the Malmesbury Electric Supply Company in 1923 with their generating station at the Postern Mill. Wessex Electricity took over the company around 1930 and the change was made from Direct to Alternating Current two years later. Below Southern Electricity Board's showroom at 18 High Street (closed in 1996 & now part of George Vets) and a cherry-picker at work outside 25 Bristol Street.

Malmesbury Chronicles 1986

Malmesbury Chronicles 1985

The factory at St Johns Bridge was built by Francis Hill in 1793 to produce woollen cloth. The quality was never good and in 1852 it was converted to make silk ribbons. This was a cyclical trade and the factory shut for long periods until it finally closed in 1941. From 1954 to 1980 it was an antiques centre and four years later it was redeveloped into flats. Before the Silk Mills closed a photograph was taken of the staff. Their names are believed to be: 1. Norah Kinchin 2. Yvette Maslen 3. Rachel Adams 4. Dora Fricker 5. Phyllis Emery 6. Betty Paginton 7. Cynthia Hayes 8. Margaret Thorne 9. Joyce Maslen 10. Beryl Martin 11. Dorothy Thompson 12. Phyllis Paginton 13. Betty Hinder 14. Dick Jones 15. Dick Bishop 16. Norah Carey 17. Arthur Paginton 18. Bill Ball 19. Bill Lay 20. Norman Savine 21. George Vanstone 22. Maurice Paginton 23. Harold Chappell 24. Tom Paul 25. Norton Shelley 26. Betty Twine 27. Margery Mills (Marion Vizor hidden) 28. Rene Baker 29. Mary Bishop 30. Rose Paginton 31. Veronica Allsopp 32. Ivy Morgan 33. Ethel Carey 34. Hazel Savine 35. Hilda Carey 36. Myra Shingles 37. Veda Maslen 38. Olive Barnes 39. Betty Vincent 40. Dorothy Vizor 41. Florrie Wood 42. Margaret Box 43. Jean Willis 44. Elsie Poole 45. Joe Hirst 46. Irene Salter 47. Rosemary Webb 48. Gwen Bailey 49. Kit Chivers 50. Ethel Paginton 51. Bessie English 52. Gladys Willis 53. May Aldridge 54. Joan Fennel 55. Lily Salter 56. Nellie Barnes 57. Cath Young 58. Gladys Jones 59. May Woodward 60. Linda Porter 61. Bessie Huff 62. Lilly Paginton 63. Betty Vizor.

David Shelley
1941

After E. K. Cole Ltd took over Cowbridge House in 1939 many changes were made and extra buildings added. Ekco merged with Pye in 1960 and 10 years later began manufacturing telephone equipment. Orders flooded in for push button phones and telephone exchange frames (above in one of the large workshops at the rear of the premises). Manufacturing moved to Glasgow in 1987 and, after a period of decline, their successor Lucent Technologies closed the site in 2002. Below - the main door into the house.

Malmesbury Civic Trust 2002

Shortly after closure Malmesbury Civic Trust were able to visit the site The exterior of the house had changed little except for the front elevation on which a large brick extension had been built in wartime. Unfortunately some parts of the interior had been stripped out but many pieces of architectural salvage such as fireplaces, doors and the main staircase (below left) were still in good condition. Above - the roof of the coach house built in 1910 with the de Bertodano family crest. Right - the Chinese-style petrol store for the house owner's cars. Below right - gears in the Mill house.

Malmesbury Civic Trust
c1930

Linolite Ltd moved to the Postern Mill (left) in 1941. This site is known to have been used from Roman times, first to make bricks & tiles, then as a slaughterhouse before becoming a corn or wool mill. In 1836 Thomas Luce turned it into a brewery. The Stroud Brewery bought the business in 1912 but closed the brewery. It became an electricity generating station in 1923 using a water turbine. Within 10 years this too closed leaving the premises empty.

Malmesbury Civic Trust 1964

Bette Richards 1990

During the war Linolite made hose clips for the military and they were ordered to leave their London factory. When hostilities ended the company remained here making lighting equipment and put up new buildings to expand their production, partly shown in the lower photo on the previous page. The Beuttell family sold the company to Rotoflex, one of Britain's leading lighting companies in 1978. They moved the factory to a new site on Tetbury Hill in 1985 (above). The Postern Mill site was redeveloped for housing called the Maltings. In turn Rotoflex merged with GTE, an American conglomerate but in 1993 the factory closed.

Dyson Ltd, formed by Sir James Dyson to produce his revolutionary bagless vacuum cleaners, moved from Bumpers Farm, Chippenham to the empty Tetbury Hill premises in 1995. Since then the campus has expanded and considerable development taken place. The modern companion view below shows the security fencing to protect the research centre and the prodigious growth of the hedge.

Malmesbury Civic Trust 2020

Pubs and Hotels

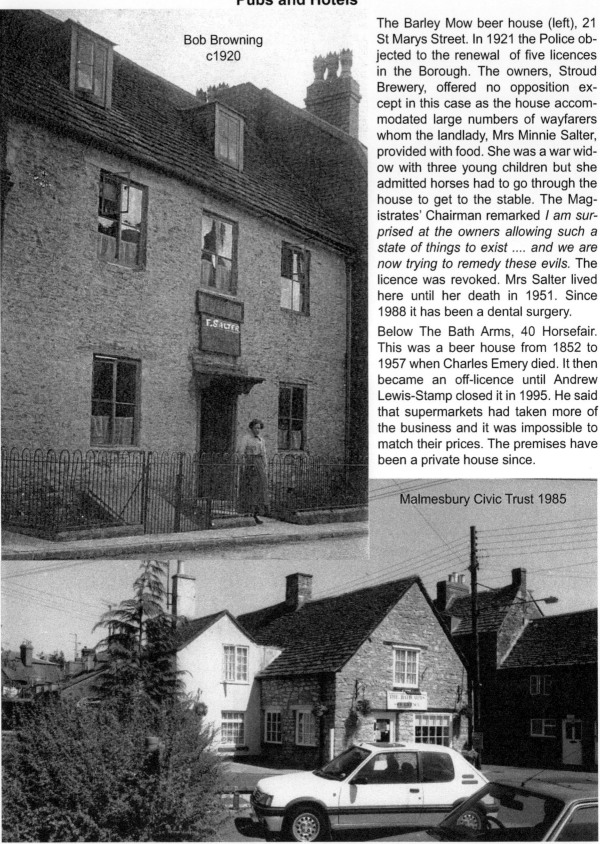

Bob Browning
c1920

The Barley Mow beer house (left), 21 St Marys Street. In 1921 the Police objected to the renewal of five licences in the Borough. The owners, Stroud Brewery, offered no opposition except in this case as the house accommodated large numbers of wayfarers whom the landlady, Mrs Minnie Salter, provided with food. She was a war widow with three young children but she admitted horses had to go through the house to get to the stable. The Magistrates' Chairman remarked *I am surprised at the owners allowing such a state of things to exist .... and we are now trying to remedy these evils.* The licence was revoked. Mrs Salter lived here until her death in 1951. Since 1988 it has been a dental surgery.

Below The Bath Arms, 40 Horsefair. This was a beer house from 1852 to 1957 when Charles Emery died. It then became an off-licence until Andrew Lewis-Stamp closed it in 1995. He said that supermarkets had taken more of the business and it was impossible to match their prices. The premises have been a private house since.

Malmesbury Civic Trust 1985

Above & right The Bear Inn 53 High Street. From 1923 William Carter was the landlord of this 17th Century coaching inn. As an Old Contemptible he warmly welcomed serv-icemen. His widow Elizabeth continued running the pub until closure in 1963. The Wilts & Gloucester Standard's local office occupied the right front 1991-2012. Since then Strakers Estate Agents have occupied it.

Below - Originally known as the Castle Inn the name changed to The Bell in 1798 and Ye Olde Bell at the start of the 20th Century.

Bob Browning
c1990

Above - the Borough Arms, 7 Oxford Street. Part of the Guildhall plot which in the 18th Century became the Nags or Boar's Head pub. Closed in 2014, the following year it became part of the Italian restaurant next door, now called La Campagna. Below - the Castle Inn, 82 the Triangle. Originally the Weavers Arms opened in 1662, the name changed to the Castle after The Bell's name change. West Country Brewers closed it in 1961 as part of an economy drive.

Bob Browning
c1955

Bette Richards c1955

Bob Browning
c1900

The Duke of York, 36 Holloway. Probably opened in the 18th Century north of the Holloway Bridge. These large premises were under-utilised so West Country Brewers replaced them with a Swedish style cedar-wood building in October 1963. For the past 15 years it has been the Spice Merchant, an Indian restaurant specialising in Kerelan food.

Malmesbury Chronicles 1985

Malmesbury Civic Trust 1964

Malmesbury Chronicles 1985

Malmesbury Civic Trust 2020

.Above - The George Hotel, 20 High Street. A coaching inn opened in the 16th Century but was rebuilt in 1768 and renamed The George. Phillip McGoldrick retired in 1964 (having been landlord for 26 years), West Country Breweries proposed to demolish the premises and build a supermarket. This failed and in 1977 it became the George Veterinary Hospital. As the business expanded so the rear of the premises changed. The pub retained the stables and carriage sheds. The Vets cleared this away to park vehicles but now extra accommodation for animals is required.

Below - Green Dragon Inn, 6 Market Cross. Built as an Abbey guest house in the 14th Century, in the early 20th Century there were plans to demolish it to improve the view of the Abbey. After the licence was lost in 1921, the licensee Robert Roper turned it into the Abbey Cafe, later the Apostle Spoon after an ancient spoon was found on the premises.

Bob Browning
c1900

The Guildhall pub, 9 Oxford Street. Fearful of conspiracies, monarchs tightly controlled buildings intended for meetings. Permission had to be obtained from King Henry IV before the Merchant's Guildhall was built c1415. The building probably extended further to the south. The site grew to include properties to the west for which the southern most part provided access. These other properties developed into the Angel Inn (now No. 5) during the 17th Century and the Nags Head (No 7) described earlier. The Warden & Freemen owns offices to the south.

In the late 17th Century the smaller Guildhall plot was divided into four tenements known as the Corner House. In 1989 there was a major refurbishment of the premises when the first floor was removed. Traces remain such as a fireplace half way up a wall. The premises became the Old Guildhall Restaurant between 1991 and 1994, then the Guildhall pub. Anti-social behaviour resulted in closure in 2013 and it was converted into an Italian restaurant the following year, now called La Campagna which also incorporates the old Borough Arms.

Malmesbury Civic Trust 1964

Malmesbury Civic Trust 2019

Malmesbury Civic Trust 1985

Malmesbury Chronicles 1986

Kings Arms Hotel, 29 High Street. Above - note the first floor brick 18th Century Georgian Assembly Room - used for public meetings and entertainments. Left - the King's Bar, to the right of the front entrance. Below - after a major refurbishment in 2019 the stables and new buildings have been converted into extra bedrooms.

Malmesbury Civic Trust 2020

Bob Browning
c1900

Bob Browning
c1900

Plough Inn, 12 Foxley Road, built in the 1840s by John Clark. A stopping off point for Commoners on their way to & from their allotments. In the 1950s Prime Minister Harold Macmillan drank here whilst visiting his daughter at Thornhill Farm. It closed on 7th February 1970 when the last publican Arthur Slade (whose family had run it since 1917) said; *People have far more things to spend their money on*.

Malmesbury Civic Trust 1964

Bob Browning
c1900

Malmesbury Civic Trust 1964

Railway Hotel, Gloucester Road.
In anticipation of the opening of the railway the hotel was built in 1875 opposite the station entrance. Its first tenant was Henry Jones who 5 years later transferred to the Kings Arms where he found fame. The next landlord was George Poole, one of the brothers who ran myrioramas. The main building is shown on the left and the stable block above. After the railway closed a competition was held in 1965 to decide on a new name and it became the Flying Monk, shown below. It closed in 1984 and International Stores obtained permitted to demolish it and build a supermarket.

Christine Jones
c1980

Malmesbury Civic Trust 1999

Above - Smoking Dog, 62 High Street. Old property deeds show these premises were open as the Greyhound Inn in 1760. Henry Long was the licensee when the railway opened which led to him withdrawing his bus service to Chippenham in 1878. A few years later the pub closed and for most of the 20th Century it was a Temperance Cafe. In 1986 it reopened as the Old Greyhound and three years later it became the Smoking Dog after a painting of one was found on the premises.

Below - The Suffolk Arms, Tetbury Hill. Originally a farmhouse for which a beer licence was obtained in 1857. The premises were extended in 1956 with a new dining room & kitchen. The restaurant earned an excellent reputation and obtained a top award in Egon Ronay's Guide of 1987. Later it became part of the Red Rooster chain and it was no longer <u>the</u> place to eat, closing in 2003. 19 houses now stand on the site, called Minot Close.

Colin Forward c1998

Malmesbury Civic Trust
c1929

The Triangle, Malmesbury.

The Three Cups, 90 the Triangle. This pub dates back to the 15th Century although the present building is 200 years later. In Elizabethan times cloth buyers stayed here when they came to purchase some of 3,000 cloths made annually. The view above seems to have been taken after a major refurbishment in the 1920s. Note the church's high boundary wall which was lowered in 1948 to improve visibility for road users. Below - the original K3 cream and red phone box installed between 1929 and 1933.

Bob Browning
c1960

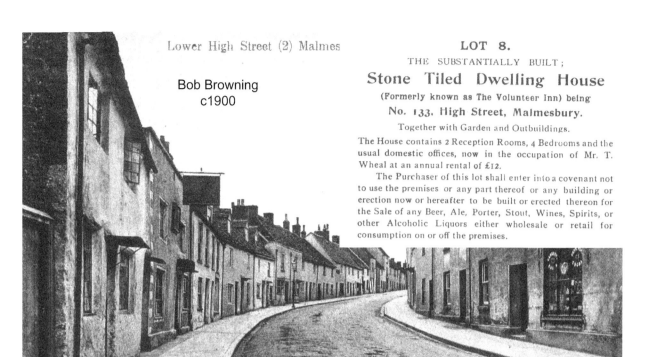

Bob Browning
c1900

LOT 8.

THE SUBSTANTIALLY BUILT;

Stone Tiled Dwelling House

(Formerly known as The Volunteer Inn) being

No. 133, High Street, Malmesbury.

Together with Garden and Outbuildings.

The House contains 2 Reception Rooms, 4 Bedrooms and the usual domestic offices, now in the occupation of Mr. T. Wheal at an annual rental of £12.

The Purchaser of this lot shall enter into a covenant not to use the premises or any part thereof or any building or erection now or hereafter to be built or erected thereon for the Sale of any Beer, Ale, Porter, Stout, Wines, Spirits, or other Alcoholic Liquors either wholesale or retail for consumption on or off the premises.

The Volunteer Inn, 133 High Street. Above is a view of the pub's sign and the sales particulars after the licence was revoked in 1921. When the Stroud Brewery sold properties a covenant prohibiting the sale of alcohol was always included.

Right - the White Lion Inn, 8 Gloucester Street seen from the Market Cross. This is on the site of an Abbey guest house dating back to the 12th Century. It then became one of the main coaching inns and a place for important public meetings. The large yard behind was where the maid servant Hannah Twynnoy was killed by a tiger in 1703. In 1855 much of the site to the west (now Gloucester House) was sold off. The narrow plot formerly occupied by the vicarage was later added on the eastern side. Whitbread sold it and the Plough at auction in 1970. Note the mirror in the distance at the corner - this was given to the Borough by Lord Suffolk in 1910.

Farmer & Stock Breeder c1935

Shops

Christine Jones c1920

Richard Boulton, the son of an agricultural labourer, worked in a bakers at the age of 13 before becoming an apprentice in Tewkesbury. By 1898 he had established a business at 24 Horsefair (the end of terrace above) in premises owned by his future mother-in-law. The bake-house adjoined the back of the house, with sacks of flour stored in the loft. After baking had finished for the day, the flour was poured through a linen sleeve down to one of the big troughs below. After the dough was mixed the various types of bread were put into tins - cottage, milk, currant, wholemeal, bran and brown. Favourites included cabbage leaf rolls (white dough wrapped in a cabbage leaf which was removed after baking leaving the imprint) and lardy cakes (dough with lard, spices, currants and raisins). The coal fired oven had a capacity of 120 loaves and was lit twice a day, three times on Saturday. Items such as meat could be roasted for customers at ½d per item. The shop sold many other items - sweets, chocolates, tea, bacon and home-made ice cream. The whole family worked hard - three daughters and the son, Fred as well as John Taylor (both shown below) did deliveries. In 1927 a new Chevrolet van was bought (below). In 1932 Richard's wife, Sarah Anne, died and after Fred left town the business closed in 1934. Richard lived at No 24 until his death in 1942.

Christine Jones 1927

Christine Jones c1927

Richard's brother Ernest also became a baker, learning his trade with his brother in Horsefair. Around 1910 he lodged with Henry Clark at Abbey Mill, using ovens in the mill building - shown on the right after having been unused for 50 years. The mill house was rebuilt in 1986 when the ovens were demolished (middle photo).

By 1914 Ernest was the owner of 96 Gloucester Road with a large bakery on site (bottom photo). As the First World War progressed more men had to be conscripted with a number of local bakers receiving their papers in 1917. The Boulton brothers were included in this batch and like their peers took their case to the local Tribunal. Both were at first given exemption but in March 1918 unusually they attended the County Tribunal together. Both asserted that their businesses could not be operated by just one - Richard stating he baked 1,350 loaves a week. It was decided that, due to his flat feet, Ernest would be exempted and in spite of his four children Richard would have to join up (Ernest was married but without children).

Ernest retired in 1937 but remained living in Gloucester Road until he died in 1965. The house was named the Old Bakehouse.

Malmesbury Civic Trust 1964

Malmesbury Chronicles 1986

Malmesbury Civic Trust 1964

Many bakers had small premises in the town until the introduction of machinery and the dominance of supermarkets. Robert Scriven had a bakehouse at 30 High Street in the 1840s. The Emery family ran bakeries for at least a century, they seem to have begun with Stephen who had premises in Gloucester Street before he moved to 30/32 High Street c1857 (left). He was followed by his son Josiah. In 1898 there was an explosion at the rear of the premises. Gas escaped through a break in a pipe outside 32 Cross Hayes and ran along an old drain into the bakery. Although the gas supply to the ovens was turned off a spark ignited it, blowing debris into Cross Hayes and badly burning Josiah. His nephew Isaac took over in 1899 but died in 1913. Isaac's widow, Annie carried on the business but she sold it c1925 to George Tanner. He retired due to ill health in 1941 when it seems to have closed for the rest of the war but reopened until the 1950s. In 1959 Barclays Bank demolished the building.

William Gladwin opened a blacksmiths at 3 Market Cross in the 1880s. His son took over c1900 but by 1911 his occupation was listed as baker, mealman and smith! He then concentrated on baking until c1935 when he sold to Marks & Werry (below). Harold then took over Malmesbury Coal Company in 1938. Marks & Werry continued until the 1970s. The ovens were at the rear of 4 Oxford Street.

Frederick Chappell was a baker and confectioner at 46 Gloucester Street from the 1860s until his death in 1920. George Tanner, who began his career at Gladwins, then took over the business and after 1925 was also running 30-32 High Street. In 1939 Herbert Avis turned Gloucester Street into a greengrocery and florist (above). In Westport David Woodman was a grocer who seems to have opened a bakery in the 1840s. His son, William, had a bakery at 84 Triangle, continued by his son (also William) until 1937. His son George and daughter Maude kept it open as a grocers until 1955 (below).

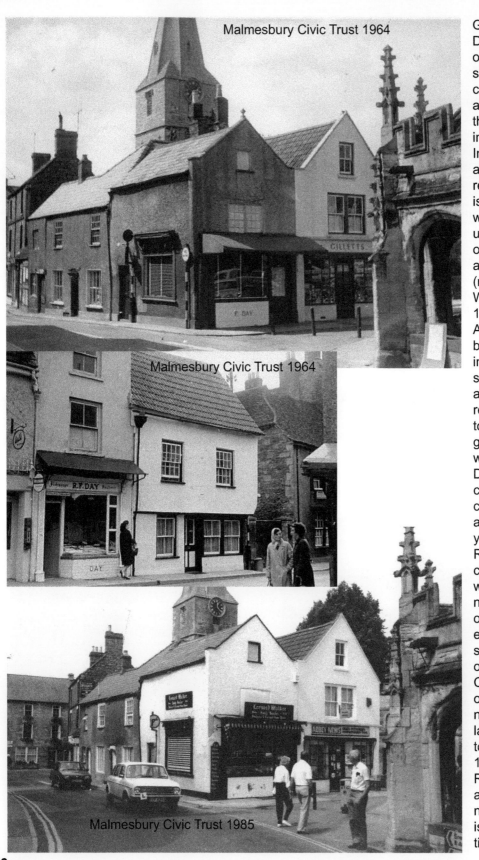

Malmesbury Civic Trust 1964

Malmesbury Civic Trust 1964

Malmesbury Civic Trust 1985

George Frederic Day, known as Fred, opened a butchers shop at 2 Market Cross c1910. In 1920 he built an abattoir just outside the Borough boundary in Park Road.

In 1919 Fred proudly advertised that he had redeemed a promise to John Wilkins, who voluntarily joined up to fight in 1914, to open a fishmongers at 4 Gloucester Street (middle photo).

When Fred died in 1948 his elder son Arthur took over the butchers until his death in 1977. The younger son, Reg, ran the abattoir and when he returned from the war took over the fishmongers. Thereafter he was known as Fishy Day. The fishmongers closed in 1979, becoming an insurance agent the following year.

Reg sold the butchers c1980 to Stuart Webb with Michael Hart running the business. One of Michael's employees, Leonard Walker, said he intended to open his own shop in Chippenham whereupon Michael opened a new business in Cricklade allowing Leonard to take over the shop in 1984. Leonard's son, Richard, joined him and now runs the business. The F Day sign is hidden by the animal tiles below the window.

The London Central Meat Company opened a shop at 18 High Street c1909. This was one of several firms importing refrigerated or chilled meat from the Americas or Antipodes and operating a chain of 'no frills' shops. Only cash was accepted and no delivery offered. The branch moved to No 4 c1930 (right) and later was renamed Baxters. William Caudell, originally from Oxford, served his apprenticeship with the London Central Meat Co and came to Malmesbury as manager in 1919. Although he moved to Bristol with them, he returned here to set up his own business at 58 High Street in 1932. After his death in 1950, his widow Edna and son Ivan carried on. They opened another shop in Little Somerford in 1956. They offered personal service and top quality meat. Edna retired in 1980 and Ivan's wife Norah joined. They closed in April 1992 (below). The business was bought by Adrian Saunders, an ex supermarket meat manager who kept on long service employees Sidney Bennett & David Scull. The shop finally closed in May 1995.

Bob Browning c1930

Bette Richards 1992

Liz Snell
c1820

Wilfred Redman, a butcher, came to Malmesbury in 1902 from Nailsworth. He first had a shop at 17 High Street which had been occupied by Eastmans Ltd, another of the 'no frills' chains. In 1907 he moved to 41 the Triangle, previously Charles Poole's butchers (left). During the First World War Wilfred appealed against conscription, stating that he employed one man and a boy. By 1939 two of his sons, John and Albert had joined him. Wilfred died in 1945 and Albert took over.

In 1952 Charles Waine bought the business for £4,000, a large sum, due to Redman's having the town's highest number of customers registered during rationing. Unfortunately Charles contracted cancer the following year so his son, Roy, had to be released from National Service. In 1973 Roy opened his Freezer Wise business at Stainsbridge Mill. No 41 was taken over by B. J. S. Brown, followed by Bryan Ballard until in 1990 Michael Thomas moved in.

51 The Triangle (below) - Mary Bick had a shop here until she died in 1917. Frances Redman, Wilfred's wife, and their daughter Nellie then ran a grocers here until 1923. Pictured are Alice Sparrow, unknown, Nellie Redman & John Redman.

Linda Hares
c1920

No 51 was bought in 1923 for Archibald Haynes who opened a fishmonger and fried fish shop. After his only son was killed in a road accident he sold the business in 1939 to Percy Pratt. His son, Gerald, followed him (above). The frying ended in 1973 and greengrocery became more important. The name changed to Open All Hours in 1986 until 1994 when David and Jane Scull renamed it Triangle Stores. This closed in 2002 and the following year Michael and Sandra Thomas moved their butchers and general store from No 41. This business has grown and light refreshments can also now be enjoyed (below).

Malmesbury Civic Trust 2020

Ted Hitchings c1908

Charles Hitchings was a carpenter and furniture dealer who lived at 63 Gloucester Road from 1902 to the 1920s. Around 1908 he built a small showroom opposite his home (above) which must have been very dangerous as the road is narrow and the door opened directly into the traffic. In 1920 he moved to a new showroom & workshop at 52 Gloucester Street and soon afterwards moved his home to 48 Gloucester Street. The showroom closed early in the war when Dennis Hatchwell turned it into a bookshop.

Charles' eldest son, Charles Leonard, known as Leonard (with his father above) opened a house furnishers at 33 High Street in 1930. It only lasted a year before he moved to 36 Gloucester Street where the business became a dealer & maker of women's clothing, upholsterer and draper, called the Fashion Centre.

.

Ted Hitchings 1930

Ted Hitchings 1931

Ted Hitchings 1935

Above - the Fashion Centre decorated for George V's Jubilee in 1935. Stock and part of the display is shown below. Leonard moved his home to Rosemead, Culver Gardens about 1947 where in a large room over the garage several girls were kept busy altering dresses. 34 Gloucester Street was Millwards shoe shop which Leonard took over in the 1940s, with a door through into the Fashion Centre. In 1958 Leonard sold the business to Beales of Bath and left town. It is now occupied by Flintstoves.

Ted Hitchings 1935

Ted Hitchings 1935

Malmesbury Chronicles 1985

David Brooks began an antiques business in 1975 at 38 Cross Hayes called Cross Hayes Antiques. The business expanded and other premises were used including the Trade Centre at 39 High Street comprising several traders selling a variety of goods and No 4 Oxford Street (left). The latter was occupied from 1984 to 1986 and Mrs Snell is shown in the doorway. In 1980 David owned 28 Horsefair living above the Horsefair Bazaar which sold Chinese china as well as bamboo and pine furniture. Importing from China became difficult so in 1983 the shop became part of Cross Hayes Antiques for a couple of years.

In 1983 the old General Post Office garage at 19 Bristol Street came up for sale and David bought it. The other shops were closed. The garage office and personnel entrance had been a small property in West Street later converted into a house called the Shoebox. In 2001 David vacated the property to concentrate on antiques fairs although between 2013 and 2019 he had a small shop at 40 High Street.

Malmesbury Chronicles 1985

Above - 19 Bristol Street after demolition. Below - the award-winning house, Chapa, has most of its accommodation on the first floor with a parking and turning area on the ground floor.

Bette Richards 1985

After the Flying Monk was closed it was demolished in 1984 and the site sold to Gateway, owned by the Dee Corporation. Dee also owned Fine Fare and initially wanted to close their store at 8 High Street but public pressure prevented this. After changes of ownership the company was rebranded as Somerfield in the 1990s. After unsuccessful attempts at expansion they were taken over by the Co-operative Group in 2009.

Bob Browning
c2000

Right - the shop at 74a the Triangle was Sealy's blacksmiths in the first half of the 20th Century. In the 1960s it became an office of North Wilts Water Board, then Triangle Design occupied it in the 1970s. After Reg Day's fish shop closed, Bryan Ballard, whose butchers was opposite, opened it as a fishmongers in 1980, managed by his 19 year old son Kevin. In 1994 the business which then sold fruit and vegetables moved to No 39. Since then 74a has been Malmesbury Glazing and now the Triangle Bookshop.

Below - William Rabbage turned No 43 the Triangle into a paper shop in 1938. The sub Post Office moved from No 39 here in the early 1950s. After various owners the shop closed in 2002 and is now the Hair Studio. No 41 was a butchers until 2004 when it became Magnifico, pizza take-away and is now Malmesbury Pizza and Kebab House.

Malmesbury Chronicles 1985

Bob Browning c2000

Malmesbury Chronicles 1986

Above - The Avon Laundrette opened at 5 Oxford Street in 1966 and provided the only self-service laundry equipment in town. When it closed in 1988 the nearest similar facilities were in Chippenham or Cirencester. Below - No 2 High Street was a grocers from the late 19th Century, run by Frederick Newman, which was taken over by the Co-operative Society until 1969. In 1973 Maureen Ockenden moved the Flower Service from Brinkworth to these premises (below). In 1988 they moved to No 4 and No 2 was redeveloped. On completion Halifax Property Services moved in until 2010. It is now the Birdcage restaurant.

Malmesbury Chronicles 1986

Michael Adye c1935

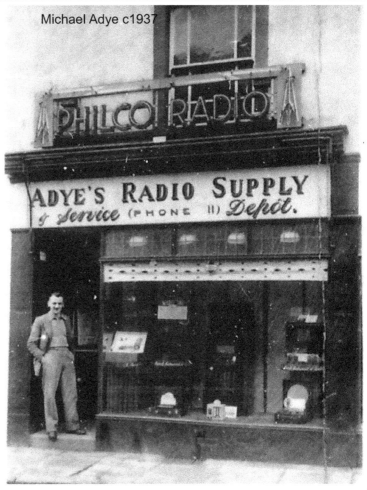

Michael Adye c1937

Alfred Adye bought the Drill Hall at the junction of Bristol Street and Bremilham Road in 1923 where he built a motor business. In 1930 he passed this on to his sons Reginald and Norman, Reg ran the motor side and Norman built up a radio business. In 1932 they bought the Gig House, on the corner of Oxford Street and Holloway.

Above - In the 1930s the Marconiphone brand and the logo G. Marconi was owned by EMI who used it for luxury radio sets. The mobile showroom proclaims the local Marconi-men were Adye Brothers in Oxford Street. Note in the background the end wall of the blacksmith in Cross Hayes Lane is on the right of the Town Hall.

Right - Reg opened a shop at 6 High Street in 1936 which remained there until 1964 when Edwin Wakefield, a competitor, refused to renew the lease. Philco, an American company, first produced rectifiers to run battery radios from the mains before manufacturing radio sets from 1926.

Malmesbury Chronicles 1986

Above - No 7 High Street was Burtons Grocers for most of the 20th Century until 1961. Edwin Wakefield then turned it into an electrical store until he moved to larger premises at No 6 around 1965. Sketchley, dry cleaners, occupied it for a couple of years before Wyles Shoes moved in until closure in 1986. In July of that year it became Oxfam, the town's first permanent charity shop (the opening above).

Below - an early view of Jones at No 17 showing off their range of goods.

Bob Browning
c1910

JONES

Gordon Williams
c1936

Above - The Decorated Motor Vehicle winner in the 1936 Carnival procession, H C Preater of Swindon's 8 synthetic white horses on an 8hp Ford car, followed by another Ford with a sign *Ford £100 Car a Wizard of the road*. Boots the Chemist are at No 19 High Street next to Olivers Lane with J E Marmont ladies fashions next door. Below - a window has been removed on the first floor of No 45 (Threshers) so a grand piano can be slid onto scaffolding before the crane lifts it to the ground for loading into the removal lorry.

Malmesbury Chronicles 1986

Housing

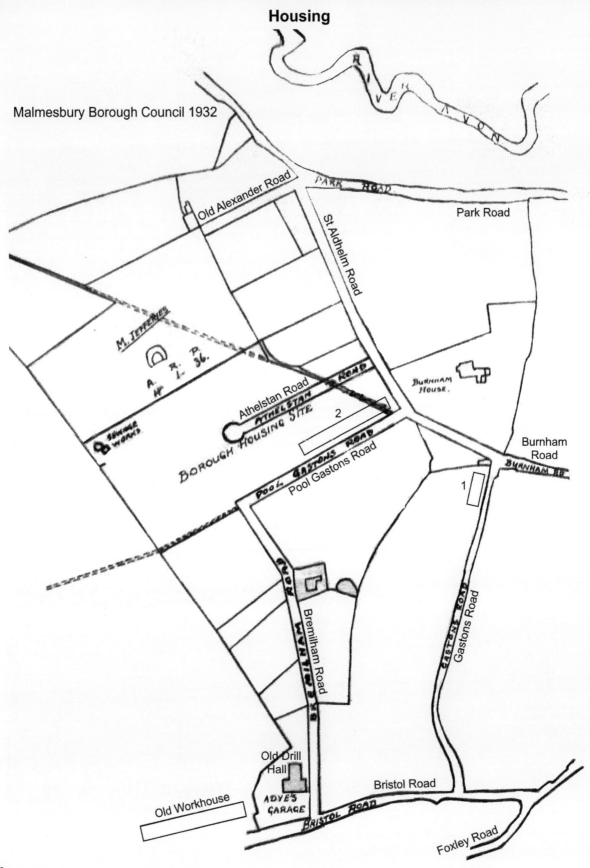

Malmesbury Borough Council 1932

Malmesbury Civic Trust 1964

There was very little private housing development until towards the end of the 20th Century. The Government first encouraged Councils to build *homes fit for heroes* after the Great War. In the 1920s there was an attempt to build on Reeds Field but this proved unsuitable. In 1931 the Council were persuaded to buy a site for £140 at the top of Gastons Road (marked 1 on the map) for 5 houses built the following year (shown above) and more land for £500 at Pool Gastons where 8 houses were built (marked 2 & shown below). These houses were lit by gas and had no electricity supply.

Malmesbury Civic Trust 1999

Secondary Modern School Field

Entrance to Allotments

N

2 Houses

Bungalow

13 14

1 2 3 4 5 6 7 8 9 10 11 12

wide path in front of terrace

Front Gardens   15 16   Front Gardens

Gardens

Adye's Garage

Entrance

Wiltshire Council took responsibility for social welfare in 1930. Three years later the Workhouse on Bristol Road closed and was sold to the Borough Council for £400. From 1936 it was made into 19 separate dwellings, known as Bremilham Terrace. Bremilham Rise with 27 Council houses replaced it after demolition in 1972

By the end of the Second World War the development of Pool Gastons and Athelstan Roads was complete. Because all the houses were for Ekco workers, materials were guaranteed. Once hostilities were over the supply of materials was restricted and the Gastons 2 scheme (houses in Alexander Road) was not completed until 1950. Below - 22 & 24 Alexander Road on the corner with Avon Road.

Malmesbury Civic Trust 1964

CORN GASTONS

The Borough Council bought 7 acres at Corn Gastons in 1944 for £650. In 1951 57 houses were planned in the biggest scheme to date. Above - Nos 50-38. Below - the Parklands old people's complex comprised six one bedroomed flats, 14 bed-sitters, a warden's flat and a communal block with kitchen and laundry. Built in 1964 the prefabs were demolished in 1990. Right - the replacement houses.

Malmesbury Civic Trust 2020

Bette Richards c1960

Liz Snell c1960

Much housing in the town was in a poor state before renovation took place in the second half of the 20th Century. Above the view from the first floor of 13 Burnham Road towards the United Reformed Church with, in the foreground, the washhouses of 18-26 taking up half of the road. Below - 32-38 Horsefair before being refurbished and the parking rearranged.

David Forward c1976

73
71
65
63

Bob Browning
c1950

Ted Hall 2007

Looking up Gloucester Road from No 81 towards the Triangle. There used to be several shops in the terrace on the eastern (left) side of the road. No 63 was Charles Hitchings' house c1901-15 (page 146), then it became Sidney Keene's refreshment rooms c1920. This was taken over in the 1920s by Mrs Taylor, followed by Arthur Butler in 1930. It was still a cafe in 1955. No 65 was used by John Bailey, tailor, from the 1880s and then by his son Robert until 1930 when Arthur Butler turned it into a pork butcher. It was still listed as a shop in the 1950s but it is unclear who ran it. No 71 was Fred & Walter Harris fishmonger in 1915-20 followed by Archibald Haynes (before moving to No 51) and Albert Radford basket work maker in the 1920s with Lillian Mustoe shopkeeper during the next decade. No 73 was Charles Gale's house, auctioneer, in 1920, then W Eatwell groceries for a short time. In the late 1920s George Bunting moved in combining his Births & Deaths Registrar duties with a confectioner's shop. It seems the shop closed after a few years. Both 71 and 73 retained their shopfronts until the millennium. The photograph on the right shows the replacement of the old metal gas pipes with yellow plastic pipes.

Mollie Raiss
1979

Mollie Raiss
1979

In the 1950s & 60s the Government encouraged Councils to demolish insanitary housing and build new - known as slum clearance. West Street seemed an ideal candidate to the Borough Council which obtained outline planning permission in 1967. However sentiment was changing and more thought was given to preserving the historic environment. So in 1974 Nos 6-30 (above and right) were listed. Work began to refurbish in 1977 but stopped after major structural problems were found.

Bette Richards c2000

Mollie Raiss
c1980

A new builder, Les Reynolds, re-started work which involved the demo-lition of the top part of the terrace (renumbered Nos 14-22 West Street - ie 11 houses re-placed 15). These were sympatheti-cally rebuilt.

In 1976 a Gen-eral Improvement Area was declared including Bristol Street, The Tri-angle, Gastons Road, Horsefair, Foundry Road and part of Glouces-ter Road. This enabled owners to obtain grants to improve their prop-erty.

Mollie Raiss
c1980

Mollie Raiss
c1980

Bob Browning
1983

The first post-war proposal to build on Reeds Farm was in 1963. The Borough Council's plan in the 1920s had failed after water saturation made it uneconomic and White Lion Park was chosen instead. In 1983 approval was given for an estate of 251 houses to be built by Persimmon Homes. This was a small Leeds based company founded only 10 years before. Further expansion has made them now the country's biggest house builder.. Above - the sign announcing the development. Below - it seems efforts were made to drain the land although problems still exist. The original farm is in the centre.

Malmesbury Civic Trust 1983

Bob Browning
1984

Work at Reeds Farm began in December 1983 and it took another six years to complete the first 251 houses. In 1990 permission was refused for 76 more as planners decided the town's infrastructure could not cope. Above - the first phase completed, 22 houses in Old Railway Close. Note the farm house still stands. Below - The Maltings, after the original contractor had become bankrupt the houses were sold off cheaply. The first 24 were sold within 2½ hours in March 1995 for prices between £50,000 and £125,000 for the large ex-clubhouse (the house with the same profile as the old malthouse).

Bette Richards 1995

A bungalow called Sorrel Garth in St Aldhelm Road was bought by a developer who gained permission to build 19 houses on the L shaped plot. Above - the bungalow is behind the sign. Below - the new houses on the road, a terrace of three, Nos 22-26 and two semi-detached houses, 28 & 30, with the entrance to 10 more houses in St Aldhelm Close between. No 32 is shown in both views.

Above - the Sorrel Garth site also fronted on to Old Alexander Road (above). The front of 1 & 3 Alexander Road is beyond the road junction. Below - A terrace of four houses called Jubilee Garden was built on the Sorrel Garth site and later another four built next to them by GreenSquare Housing on the site of a block of garages.

Malmesbury Civic Trust 2020

Above - Park Road looking towards A C Nurden (now Buildbase) and the road to Brokenborough. On the left is part of the abattoir which closed in 1998. Below - the right foreground shows the wall of 43 Park Road, with 45, a gap where it is intended to erect a bridge over the river, 47 and 49. To the left 20 & 22 Park Road, a garage block and 16 Park Close.

Malmesbury Civic Trust 1999

Malmesbury Civic Trust 2020

David Hendry, who had been a top salesman for Athelstan Garage, set up his own business in barns at Punters Farm, Park Road in 1980 (above). Three years later the business expanded after becoming Subaru agents. In 2007 the business moved to Filands but after David's death in 2019 it closed the following year. Six houses called Kingfisher Mill were built on the old site (below). Between the two blocks there is access to farm buildings on the other side of the river (right).

Malmesbury Civic Trust 2020

Malmesbury Civic Trust 2001

Bette Richards
2001

Cathay, a bungalow in Bristol Street next to the Old School House, was built c1920 by William Rich. He was a keen horseman and had stables on the site. After he died it was bought by Fred Day, the butcher with a shop at the Market Cross. On the death of Fred's son Reg in 1999 the property was sold for development. 12 houses were built on the site in 2002, called Crab Tree Close (below).

Malmesbury Civic Trust 2020

After the Filands School was vacated permission was obtained for 168 houses on the site. Persimmon Homes began building in 2006. Above - the view before work started with the Dyson factory just visible above the traffic island. Below - the junction of Tetbury Hill and Dyson now has a mini-roundabout. Cars are parked on the stub road to the left where school buses had previously waited.

Sheila Dent 2011

These four photographs illustrate the progress of part of the Bloor Homes development of 180 houses on Filands. The viewpoint is at the end of Webbs Way looking north. It is pleasing to note that much of the long hedge shown above has been retained although there are now large gaps for roads. The final illustration shows 29-53 (odds) Snell Avenue.

Sheila Dent 2016

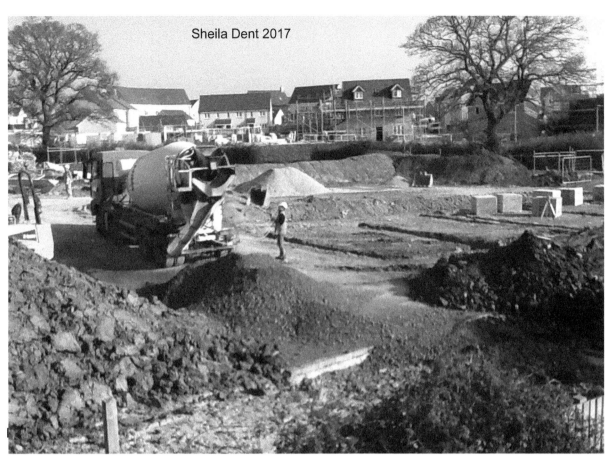

Sheila Dent 2017

Sheila Dent 2019

Events

Malmesbury Chronicles
1887

The newly formed Borough Council arranged the town celebration of Queen Victoria's Golden Jubilee. At 10.20 on 22 June 1887 a procession comprising Malmesbury Brass Band, Yeomanry, Volunteers, Police, Mayor and Corporation, various Benefit Societies and the Somerford Fife & Drum Band formed at the Silk Factory. They marched to the Abbey for a service. At 2pm a cold dinner was served at 30 tables in Cross Hayes (above and below). 1,500 people enjoyed this free treat. Later there was a tea for children and sports on the Wortheys. Below the rear of the George Hotel can be seen with bay windows and the rear of Garlick's butchers used as their slaughterhouse.

Malmesbury Civic Trust
1887

George Hotel

Garlick's butcher

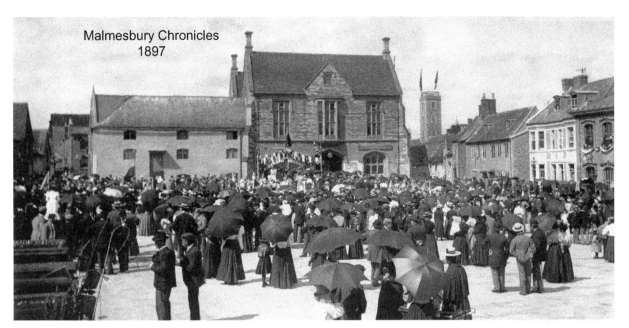

Malmesbury Chronicles
1897

Queen Victoria's Diamond Jubilee in 1897 was celebrated more lavishly. On Sunday 20 June there was a service in the Abbey at which the Mayor, William Forrester, wore the gold chain of office for the first time. On Tuesday 22 June *no town celebrated the reign more loyally or royally as the ancient borough.* At 10am a procession moved from St Johns Street, up the High Street and into Cross Hayes where the dignitaries sat on a platform and speeches were made (above). Lunch in the Council Chamber, Silver Street, followed. A children's tea, entertainment, sports and dancing were provided near Joseph Poole's Verona House, Gloucester Road. On Wednesday a procession of business vehicles (below) made its way from Cross Hayes to Verona House. In the background an arch over the road can be seen, decorated with evergreens, coloured flowers and flags.

Malmesbury Chronicles
1897

Athelstan Museum
1902

Malmesbury Chronicles
1902

The Coronation of King Edward VII took place on 9 August 1902, having been postponed when the King was ill in June. It was reported that nearly all the town's buildings were nicely decorated (above). The Mayoress, Catherine Forrester, decorated the Market Cross with festoons of evergreens and roses, illuminated with fairy lamps and Chinese lanterns. A procession marched along the High Street to a service in the Abbey. At the end they paraded through the principal streets. At 1pm 150 prominent citizens and clergymen sat down to a champagne lunch. At 5pm the Mayoress presented every child under 15 with a medal after which they enjoyed tea and sports. In Cross Hayes there were amusements which the Mayor, William Forrester, and the Corporation watched from a platform by the Malthouse (below).

Malmesbury Chronicles
1902

Athelstan Museum
1905

Henry Howard, 19th Earl of Suffolk, married Daisy Leiter on 26 December 1904 at her home in Washington. The couple had met just months before in India. She had inherited a large fortune. They crossed the Atlantic and at 2.40pm on 12 January arrived at Malmesbury station. They were welcomed by a large crowd and inspected the Volunteer Company (above). They then drove to the Market Cross where another large crowd awaited them together with Mayor Thomas Reed and Corporation. Below - the Earl responds to the Mayor's address whilst journalists make notes. The Volunteers in the centre foreground have shouldered rifles.

Bob Browning
1905

Malmesbury Civic Trust
1910

On 11 May 1910 George V was proclaimed King. A procession began at the Council Chambers, Silver Street and made its way to the old Courthouse, St Johns Street where the proclamation was read, the Royal Salute given and the National Anthem played. The next stop was the Market Cross where, after the proclamation, the large crowd sang the National Anthem (above). This ceremony was repeated at the Triangle. Although Edgar Basevi photographed the Coronation celebrations on 22 June 1911 no copies have been found. Below - The Malmesbury Boy Scout Troop was formed on 8 February 1910 thanks to the generosity of the de Bertodano family of Cowbridge House. It was led by Sgt William Perry (on the right), assisted by Arthur Ponting (left). Within a short time 55 boys had joined.

Kim Power c1910

Liz Snell
1912

In 1909 the Mayor, Joe Moore, wanted to refurbish the Market Cross and persuaded the Earl of Suffolk to chair the fund-raising committee. Harold Brakspear, who oversaw the restoration of the Abbey shortly before, was chosen as architect. The work was done by Robert Rudman of Chippenham using the best Box stone to renew many of the pinnacles, the statues around the top and other parts of the structure. The fresh stonework can be seen on the right.

On the afternoon of Friday 26 April 1912 a large crowd assembled around the Cross which Scoutmaster Perry and the Boy Scouts had veiled. The mass of people made it impossible for the journalists to use the table set up for their note taking. First the Lord Bishop of Bristol, George Forrest Browne, who was keenly interested in the town and had instigated the repair of the Abbey, made the introduction (above). Then the Countess of Suffolk unveiled the monument and handed it over to the Mayor. Speeches were made by Mayor James Jones, the Earl of Suffolk, Aldermen Thomas Hinwood and Joe Moore before the official party went off to a reception. A brass plaque, which seems to be missing, was erected saying *This Market Cross was restored by public subscription during 1910-1912, through the exertions of Mr Joe Moore*.

Liz Snell
1912

Athelstan Museum
1922

During August 1922 Queen Mary holidayed at Westonbirt House, the home of Sir George and Lady Holford. Whilst there she visited many places in the area and on Saturday 22nd came to Charlton Park and Malmesbury Abbey. She was accompanied by Sir George and met by the vicar, Revd. Charles Paterson (above). Below - it is interesting to note that Charles Hitchings furniture showroom advertised tyres!

Liz Snell
1922

Visit of H.M. The Queen to Malmesbury Abbey. Aug. 1922

On 23 June 1924 King Athelstan's Millenary was celebrated. The day began at 11am with a service in the Abbey. At 1.30pm *the largest and most representative of any procession within living memory* formed up at the Secondary School and moved to the Triangle. Joined there by the band and the Royal Ancient Order of Buffaloes who laid a wreath at the War Memorial, they proceeded to the Market Cross and on to Ingleburn Manor (Burton Hill House). Above - St John of Beverly's cohort cross the Town Bridge. At 2.45 *Athelstan, a Pageant Play* written by Mabel Kerry, Secondary School Headmistress and Miss P N Maby, Assistant Mistress, was performed by a large company, mainly their pupils. Dance sequences and songs formed part of the six Episodes. Tea followed this performance then the Boy Scouts portrayed the scenes in Malmesbury when the warriors returned from battle and were rewarded by Athelstan. The Pageant was repeated at 7pm whilst the official party enjoyed dinner in the Town Hall!

Jon England 1930

Bob Browning
1939

Above - In 1930 Boswell & Wombwell's Circus set up in Cross Hayes. Bill Wheadon, the hairdresser at 36 High Street was challenged to cut someone's hair in the lions den. George Gay, landlord of the George Hotel, had previously drunk a bottle of beer with lions so he accepted. Unfortunately this time the trainer forbade any alcohol. The performance was repeated in the evening.

In the late 1930s Bernard Basevi was well known here as a conjuror and entertainer, using the name Athelstanio. In the 1939 Carnival one of the most thrilling sideshows was when he was manacled and thrown into the river. His hands and arms were chained and padlocked, he climbed into a sack which was tied in the presence of a large crowd. The sack was thrown from a plank into the river by the Town Bridge. After a while he surfaced and swam to the bank. Previously sawdust had been spread on the water and Bernard had manoeuvred under the bridge where he paused to raise the tension. On the left he is shown before the performance with the Mayor, Dr Bernulf Hodge (with the shooting stick). Bernard died in 1941 after his plane ditched in the North Sea.

Liz Snell
1940

Above - Queen Mary spent the war at Badminton. She frequently visited the town. In October 1940 she inspected the Home Guard and is shown leaving the Abbey. Other occasions included inspecting the parade at War Weapons Week in 1941 and the Ekco factory in 1943. Below - Ekco arranged a party for their employees' children in 1942 at the Cowbridge works and this became an annual event. After the war all local children were invited with coaches to transport them. Up to 400 attended. Following redundancies the parties stopped in the late 1970s but one took place in 1981 with 100 children.

Roger Lewis
1950

Liz Snell
1955

Above - the Queen Mother frequently passed through Malmesbury on her way to Cheltenham races but in March 1955 she made a visit to the Abbey where the vicar, Revd. Arthur Beaghen and Mayor Dennis Morse met her. There was no announcement but a small crowd gathered and children were released from schools. Below - One of the most popular annual social events was the Burton Hill fete held in June or July between 1947 and the School's closure in 2007. Many side shows, bands and other events drew large crowds on a Saturday afternoon. Ekco and the RAF regularly supported the event and large sums were raised starting from £200 to £1160 in 1970 and £3500 in 1984. Jack Warner, who played Dixon of Dock Green, opened it in 1959.

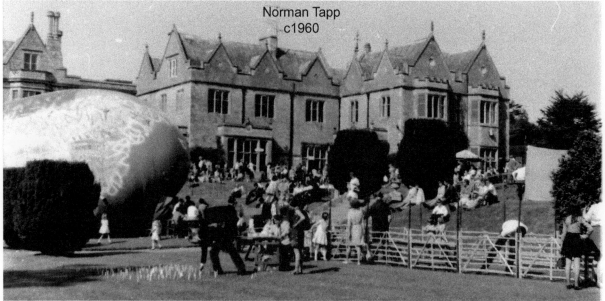

Norman Tapp
c1960

Bette Richards 1960

Malmesbury suffers from flooding from time to time. In December 1960 two inches of rain in 24 hours on top of a period of steady rainfall resulted in the worst floods for many years. Above - the situation at St Johns Bridge and below near the Holloway Bridge with the Avon Caravan site just above the water.

Bette Richards 1960

Bob Browning
1962

An RAF Royal Tournament display depicting the 'first' flight in 1506 inspired Max Woosnam (above left), to write and tell them of Elmer's flight in 1010. As a result the 1962 Carnival was enlivened on Friday 7th and Saturday 8th September by the Display Team re-enacting Elmer's flight but on a zip wire from the Abbey. A rehearsal is shown below. Junior Technician Bernard Collins took the lead role in a son et lumiere involving around 50 characters with a commentary by Revd. Arthur Beaghen. More than 5000 saw the spectacle. Fortunately on this occasion Brother Elmer did not break his legs!

Jim Gilmore 1962

Malmesbury Town Council 1980

Princess Anne made an official visit to the town on 27 May 1980 to help celebrate the 1100th Anniversary of the first Charter. At the time she was often seen using shops here from her home at Gatcombe. On this occasion she was welcomed by the Lord Lieutenant and Mayor Edwin Wakefield. In the Town Hall members of the Town Council and Niebull Council were introduced. The party then moved to the Old Courthouse, the Almshouses, up the High Street (above) to the Abbey. In Cloister Garden she unveiled a plaque with Councillor Roy Cooper, the Anniversary Committee Chairman and the Mayor looking on.

Malmesbury Town Council 1980

Malmesbury Civic Trust 2000

Floods struck the Lower High Street and Staines Bridge in 1963, 1965, 1967 (twice), 1968 and 1969. Work to alleviate the flooding risk was carried out in the 1970s at Abbey Mill and St Johns Bridge but floods still occurred in 1971, 1977 and 1979 (twice). 1984/5 saw larger works at Cowbridge weir, Holloway, Baskerville and Daniels Well. At Christmas 1985 32mm of rain was quickly followed by another 30mm which caused the floodplain at Daniels Well to flood for the first time. Minor problems occurred in 1992 but the town escaped much damage until January 1999 when again the worst floods in living memory happened. Further devastation came about in October 2000, St Johns Street shown above and below at Goosebridge.

Malmesbury Civic Trust 2000

Derek Tilney 2001

The Queen and Prince Philip visited Chippenham, Calne and Malmesbury on 7 December 2001. They first went to the Town Hall. Above George Kelsall, John Kerslake, the Prince, the Queen, the Lord Lieutenant (Sir Maurice Johnston) and Mayor John Bowen examine the Warden & Freemen's maces. They were entertained to lunch before walking to the Abbey, pausing at the Market Cross (below) to sign photographs for the Royal British Legion. The vicar, Revd. David Littlefair, led a short service before they departed to visit the Dyson factory for a demonstration of their products.

Malmesbury Civic Trust 2001

Malmesbury Civic Trust 2003

In October 2003 Hannahs Sandiford, Farci, Ekbateni, Mitchell, Lake, Watson, Turner, Roberts and Garry, all aged between four and ten joined Revd. Peter Yacomeni & Mayor Charles Vernon at a ceremony to commemorate 300 years since the death of Hannah Twynnoy who was killed by a tiger. 9 Regiment Royal Logistic Corps was granted the Freedom of Malmesbury in June 2010. They marched from the Triangle War Memorial to Cross Hayes where campaign medals for their recent tour in Afghanistan were presented.

Robert Peel 2010

Bette Richards 2012

Once again there were major floods in 2012 which had coverage throughout the world. This led to the Environment Agency agreeing to carry out work in conjunction with riparian owners. The Old Corporation removed the base of the long demolished gasometer and the Town Council cleared Cucking Stool Mead to improve flow to St Johns Bridge. The river bed beneath the bridge was dredged. A scheme to protect properties nearby is still being discussed. Above - the Memorial Gates and below the Old Corporation's houses next to St Johns Bridge.

Bette Richards 2012

Graham Cooke 2013

WOMAD (World of Music, Arts and Dance) was founded in 1980 and has held festivals in the UK since 1982. After many years at Reading the main event site moved to Charlton Park in 2007. During the last weekend in July thousands descend on the town to attend, many camping on site (above). There are at least five stages to showcase artists from all over the world together with local acts including some from our schools. The musicians also hold workshops involving dance, musical instruments and discussions, as well as painting, circus skills, graffiti, modelling and story telling for children. International food and goods are sold. In 2020 the festival took place online.

Graham Cooke 2019

Malmesbury Civic Trust 2020

2020 will be remembered for the Covid-19 pandemic. On 23 March the Government announced severe restrictions shutting most businesses and telling people to remain at home. Few ventured into Malmesbury town centre for many weeks. After the number of disease-related deaths peaked in April; restrictions were reduced - non-essential shops could reopen from 15 June, pubs, cafes, cinemas and hairdressers from 4 July. In the upper High Street parking was banned from 10 June to give pedestrians more room and to allow for queues outside shops. Above the High Street with a short queue outside the Old Bakehouse to the left of the lorry unloading. Below an Information Tower by the Market Cross.

Malmesbury Civic Trust 2020

Sports

John Smith
1926

Malmesbury Bowls Club was formed in 1908 when it separated from the Cricket Club. Early games were played on the cricket pitch after matches but soon land was rented on the Kings Arms meadow, north of Holloway, now occupied by the Vicarage. In 1912 the club moved to the present ground, Little Mead, Baskerville, leased from Tom Rich. Above are club members in 1926. Back row: E Parsonson, J Halliday, D Cookson, J Riddick, J Perry, H Iles, G Preston, H Halfacree, F Taylor, G Bunting, E Bowring, J Gregory, W Carter, A Goddard, S Allen. Front row: Mrs E Allen, Mrs J Matthews, Mrs Miles, Mrs H Bailey, E Boulton, W McClure, J Curtis, H Cameron, H Farrant, J Matthews, G Deadman, S Pearce, E Allen, A Greenfield, H Bailey, W Caudell, A Adye, Dr J Maitland-Govan. On 16th August 1968 the club played a Diamond Jubilee Match against the Wiltshire County Executive. Below is Malmesbury's team. Back row: F J Poole, A Haylock, H Vizor, R Carey, H Poole, C Purbrick, D Ledbury, H Bailey. Middle row: J Champion, G Paterson, G Maidment, K Stoneham, G Exton, J Aylward, Front row: R Daniels, B Litton, H Avis (President), R Avis (Captain), C Punter, C Paginton.

John Smith
1968

Colin Hicks 2000

During the early years at the new green maintenance costs were high as were the annual fees so it is likely the 1926 photo shows the whole membership. Following the Second World War numbers increased and benefactors like Alfred Beuttell (a keen player and President for four years) enabled the site to be bought. In 1964 a new pavilion was built. Much competitive success was enjoyed in the 1970s including winning the National Club Two Fours in 1976, only the second English trophy to be won in Wiltshire. The river was diverted to add two extra rinks and the pavilion extended (to the left below). Unfortunately as the site is nearly surrounded by the river it has frequently flooded as illustrated above. In 2020 the playing area has been raised and a synthetic surface laid to minimise future damage and improve drainage. After Covid-19 restrictions were eased a match on 18 July 2020 is shown below.

Malmesbury Civic Trust 2020

Malmesbury Civic Trust
c1949

Malmesbury Boxing Club was formed in 1923 but closed down within a year. In 1947 Malmesbury Junior Boxing Club began in the Social Centre, Ingram Street. One of the founders was Charles Jones (the large man in the centre above) who had also been involved before. Although they were given a training facility in Linolite's old malthouse interested waned and the club wound up in 1961. In 1977 the efforts of Fred Wartnaby and Eric Lewis resulted in the Malmesbury and Brokenborough Boxing Club. Initially based in the British Legion Club, Ingram Street, they moved to the Cartmell Centre, Gloucester Road in 1986 (below). Unfortunately not all of the names of the young men are known but the adults are: Tony Stannard, coach (centre), front row: Peter Langdon, Harry da Costa, Fred Wartnaby, Les Allen and Dave Harvey.

Mike Rees
c1986

Mike Rees
1987

The club raised £20,000 to build a new clubhouse on land leased from the Town Council next to the football ground (left with Tony Stannard). Unfortunately this ground has flooded on many occasions until in 2011 Mrs Sam Winstone, mother of a young boxer, helped raise another £20,000 to rebuild above flood level (below).

Tony Stannard, a former successful amateur boxer, moved from London to Malmesbury. For 30 years he was responsible for nurturing many young boxers. In 2006 he was awarded an MBE.

The club has had many successful boxers and the careers of just two have been selected.

Below right - Tony Falcone from Chippenham turned professional in 1990 contesting 20 super featherweight bouts with 12 wins. He fought for a Commonwealth title until retiring in 1996 when he became assistant club coach.

Below - Joe Hughes was born with Erb's palsy. In an effort to overcome a shortened and weaker right arm he took up boxing as a form of physiotherapy. He made his professional debut in 2010 and so far of 23 fights he has won 17. He held the European super-lightweight title in 2018/9.

Malmesbury Civic Trust 2020

Mike Rees
2019

Unfortunately Tony Stannard died in 2017 but Mike Rees, a former amateur boxer, was able to take over. The club continues to prosper, many juniors and women train here including four national novice champions and three junior finalists. Its reputation attracts members from a wide area. Above - the refurbished gym.

Malmesbury Cricket Club 1900

Early editions of the Wilts & Gloucester Standard in 1838 reported cricket matches being played by Malmesbury Cricket Club. By 1867 they were playing on the Wortheys. The photo above was taken in 1900 at a match with Bristol Licenced Victuallers and includes representatives of prominent families including Duck, Forrester, Alexander and Ratcliffe. However the club closed in 1911 and was not re-formed until 1932. It was not until after the war that the club began to prosper. St Aldhelms Mead was used from 1947 until a return to the Wortheys in 1951. Trevor Richards not only worked hard to restore the pitch but took over as Captain after Jack Ellett's untimely death in 1954. The 1953 first XI is shown below. Back row; Pat Norris, Ron Pierce, John Box, Jim Pike, Trevor Richards, Max Lloyd, George Ockwell, Ted Blanchard & Jim Gilmore. Middle row; Bert Duxbury, Ron Jones, Jack Ellett, Les Hinder & Frank Ferne. Front Brian Box.

Jim Gilmore 1953

Malmesbury Cricket Club c1955

Above - the vicar, Revd. Beaghen, held Sunday evening services on the Wortheys. Between the 1960s and 80s the club was playing 'well above its weight' - in 1968 an augmented side took on the Worcester County team, In 1972 they won the Wiltshire League and the following year the Western League (which included Bath, Cardiff, Cheltenham & Gloucester). 1982 & 1985 saw them winners of the Famous Grouse Western League. Below - practice on the ground with Abbey House, the Abbey and the Cliff as a backdrop.

Colin Forward c1980

Malmesbury Victoria Football Club 1948

Malmesbury Football Club played their first match in November 1895 against Calne winning 4-0. The next match against Chippenham United was lost 2-4 as *the home team knew nothing of the match until the morning's post and were short of some of their best men!* At the beginning of the 20th Century the name Malmesbury Town was in use. After the Great War the club joined the Vale of White Horse (VWH) League but in 1936 attendances were poor, no one wanted to be an official and the club was wound up. After the next war the Town club was re-formed and another called Ekco Colts started. In 1947-8 the Town won the VWH Cup. Above - the team at Corn Gastons with the old Workhouse as a backdrop. Back row: Joe Bailey, Dave White, Les Bick, Jock Patterson, Jack Grundon, Dicky Bird, Bill Barron, Ken Haylock, Cecil Gregory, Albert Haylock. Front row: Arthur Rogers, Mike Hulbert, Jock Baker, Dave Vaughan (captain), Theo Douglas, George Carey, Tom Clancey. Below - the winning teams of 1973-4.

Malmesbury Victoria Football Club 1974

Malmesbury Victoria Football Club 1974

The Town won the VWH Cup again in 1948-9 and the Ekco Colts, renamed Malmesbury United, joined the Town Club in 1951. The lack of a permanent home caused great difficulties. Since the war they played on the Four & Twenty Steps field, Milbourne, Backbridge, Corn Gastons, Bristol Road and Whiteheath Farm, Corston until in 1970 they moved to the Flying Monk ground, the old market site owned by the Borough Council. In 1973-4 the 1st team won Wiltshire League Division 1 and the 2nd team Division 2, the first time this had happened. The teams are shown on the previous page with Fred Wartnaby, the Chairman on the extreme left. Above - the team managers collect the trophies: Pete Brown, Dave Picter, Dave Chivers, Mike Hodge & Don Rogers (1st team manager). A year later the club merged with Swindon Victoria. Below - the ground has flooded many times in the past 50 years which has caused severe financial problems for the club and the difficulty of improving facilities has prevented promotion. The first team now plays in the Hellenic League Division 1 West with the second team in the Wiltshire Senior League Premier Division.

Wiltshire Police 2020

Gordon Williams
1906

The photo above suggests the Malmesbury Tennis Club closed in 1906 as it is marked FINIS. Unfortunately the only person named is the gentleman on the right - Percy Jackson, a High Street outfitter described as 24 years old and a tennis enthusiast. The club was re-formed and players from 1911 are shown below.
Top: Miss N Sharpe, Mr & Mrs P Bower. H Gladwin, Miss Curtis with P Curtis & K Cameron in front. Bottom Back row: E Basevi, Miss Bartholomew, T Clerk, Miss G Adye, Mr Hope, Miss G Thomas, W Vaughan, Miss E Woodman. Middle row: Miss I Adye, J Adye, Miss G Altie, H Hinwood, Miss M Woodman, S Adye, Miss N Bower, A Greenman, ? Front F Riddick, Miss E Riddick, E Ratcliffe.

In the first decade of the 20th Century courts were rented from Thomas Henry at the Gables, Crudwell Road. Competitive matches were played against clubs from other towns seemingly winning more often than losing. In 1922 new courts were prepared at the Gables and 78 players entered an 'American' tournament (every player plays every other player). In 1935 David Adye, Richard Cole, Donald Clark and Gilbert Guest, all aged under 21, bought land on behalf of the club on Tetbury Hill for £35. Clinker was bought from the GWR and brought by cart to the site to form the foundation for three hard courts. Play began the following year. At the end of the war hard work was required to restore the courts. In the 1950s membership dropped to 40 and as an inducement the public were able

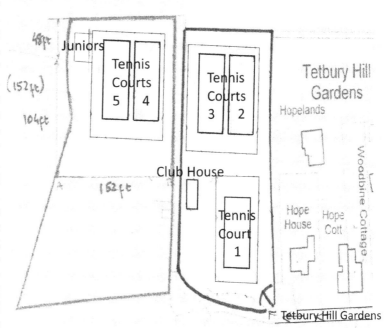

to play for 2s 6d per game. New material - Red Griselda - was used to resurface the courts in 1958. A pavilion (an ex-builder's hut) with a dressing room for the first time was erected in 1961. In 1970 the club joined the Chippenham and District League and the Ladies team were top in the first season. The Men had to progress through 3 divisions before they won Division 1 in 1974. In 1988 one court was provided with an all-weather surface to enable play throughout the year. Since then there has been considerable further investment - the other two courts were resurfaced by 1995, floodlights for two courts installed in 2004 and extra land to the west acquired in 2009. The plan above shows the present layout with two new courts and a facility for children on the new ground. There are still plans for a new club house to replace the old one which is showing its age. Below is a view from Court 4 towards the original site.

Malmesbury Civic Trust 2020

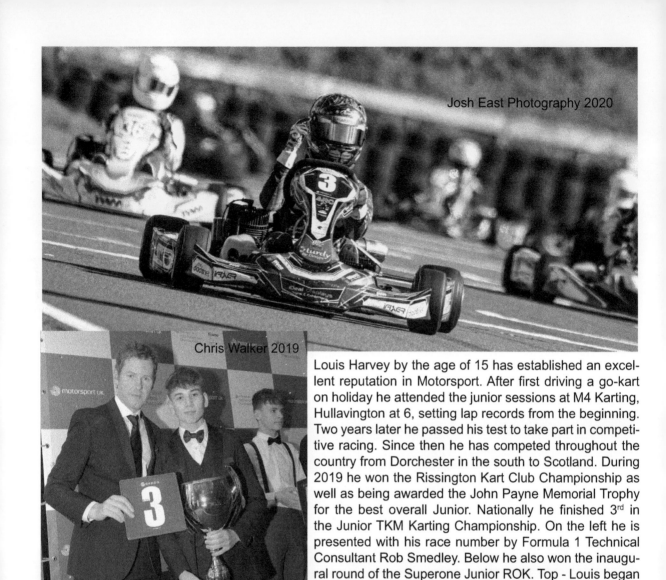

Josh East Photography 2020

Chris Walker 2019

Louis Harvey by the age of 15 has established an excellent reputation in Motorsport. After first driving a go-kart on holiday he attended the junior sessions at M4 Karting, Hullavington at 6, setting lap records from the beginning. Two years later he passed his test to take part in competitive racing. Since then he has competed throughout the country from Dorchester in the south to Scotland. During 2019 he won the Rissington Kart Club Championship as well as being awarded the John Payne Memorial Trophy for the best overall Junior. Nationally he finished 3rd in the Junior TKM Karting Championship. On the left he is presented with his race number by Formula 1 Technical Consultant Rob Smedley. Below he also won the inaugural round of the Superone Junior ROK. Top - Louis began the delayed 2020 season winning at Shenington.

Chris Harvey 2019

Skateboarding has been a popular pastime of the town's young people for a long time. In 1997 the Malmesbury Skateboarders and Riders Group was formed hoping to build an outdoor skate park. Consultation with residents and noise tests ruled out several locations. In 2004 a few ramps were bought for the Cartmell Centre but a better solution remained the top priority for youth. Eventually discussions with the Youth Service and Wiltshire Council led to plans to build the first indoor concrete skatepark in the UK, at a cost of £250,000. Planning permission was granted in 2012 and building began the following year on the 230 square metre extension to the Youth Centre in Gloucester Road (now the Riverside Centre). August 2013 saw the park open its doors for the first time to host an opening day competition attended by over 100 people. Unfortunately due to spending cuts the Youth Centre was closed in January 2014 together with the park.

Matt Wigley and Alan Holt then formed the Malmesbury Skate Park Group and sought to take over the skatepark. In 2015 the group became a charity and reopened the park. It has been open most evenings to provide free of charge skate sessions, coaching and a positive sporting activity. Funded by donations and with ten volunteer organisers it provides the town with a facility which is the envy of many bigger towns and cities – a non commercial, free, indoor concrete skatepark.

Above - Sam Vugts, Jasper Neale, Martin West, Matt Wigley and Alan Holt inside the park at its reopening and before the installation of ramps. Right - a young skateboarder demonstrates.

Index